SPIRITUAL MESSAGES FROM

METATRON

LIGHT IN THE TIMES OF CRISIS

HS Press

SPIRITUAL MESSAGES FROM

METATRON

LIGHT IN THE TIMES OF CRISIS

RYUHO OKAWA

HS PRESS

Original title: *Metatron no Reigen-Kiki no Jidai no Hikari*
HS Press is an imprint of IRH Press Co., Ltd.
Tokyo
ISBN 13: 978-1-943928-19-4
ISBN 10: 1-943928-19-3
Cover Image: NicoElNino/Shutterstock.com

The opinions of the space being in this book do not necessarily reflect those of Happy Science Group.
For the mechanism behind spiritual messages, see the end section.

Contents

Preface 9

Spiritual Messages from Metatron
Light in the Times of Crisis

1 Asking Metatron about the Various Issues Afflicting the Earth 14

2 The Truth about the Coronavirus Pandemic and China's Strategy

What is behind the G7 countries' growing condemnation of China 19

The crisis that will be brought about by the idea, "vaccination will calm things down" 24

3 Recognize the True Nature of China

Why did coronavirus suddenly spread in Vietnam? 29

Will the vaccination measures end in a cat-and-mouse game? 32

A state that resembles a giant Aum cult has emerged 36

What is China's strategy to break the anti-China coalition? 39

China knows all about the weaknesses of democracies 43

4 Japan's Moves Hold the Key to the World

Don't repeat Europe's response at the time of Hitler's emergence 46

Who are the "key players" in putting China under siege? 52

What was the opinion of the guardian spirit of Prime Minister Suga, who visited Ryuho Okawa? 56

Why does Prime Minister Suga want to push forward with the Tokyo Olympic Games? 59

The fifth coronavirus wave and how it may affect the Winter Olympic Games in China 61

5 Observing the Current Political Situation in Japan

Will we see the return of the year 2009 when the ruling party lost in a landslide? 64

Japan's "socialist policies" have made it impossible to distinguish between the ruling party and the opposition parties 68

Put various thoughts in perspective for Japan, which is in the process of sinicization 72

6 The Current State of the Earth as Seen from the Cosmic Perspective

How to confront the forces that are developing hell via China 75

Why Japan's space mission lags far behind 80

The situation in the Middle East and the future of the "decarbonized society" 84

Will the royal family and the imperial family be able to survive? 86

Will religions join their forces from now on? 88

The time has come to put an end to the allergy to religion 93

7 A Message from the "Gods of Genesis"

Why must we make the world on earth the place where the good side wins? 96

Create a "free market of thoughts" in China 99

The time when we need to create something new has come 101

How can we subdue the pride of the earthlings who have become so conceited? 102

It's time to correct the false notion of separation of church and state 106

The influence of evil aliens behind the Second World War 110

What is expected of Japan now? 114

Afterword 117

About the Author 121
What Is El Cantare? 122
What Is a Spiritual Message? 124
About Happy Science 128
About Happiness Realization Party 130
Happy Science Academy Junior and Senior High School 131
Contact Information 132
About IRH Press 134
Books by Ryuho Okawa 135
Music by Ryuho Okawa 145

In this book, there are a total of three interviewers from Happy Science, symbolized as A, B, and C, in the order that they first appear.

Preface

Recently, there were heavy rainfalls in Germany, resulting in severe flooding. The Rhine River overflowed, and over 200 people were reported killed. The Chinese official media saw this and mockingly said, "Germany is just like one of the developing countries." Soon after, China was also hit by heavy rains that affected more than three million people. In the Yellow River basin, people, cars, and houses were swept away. This time, the Chinese government announced it was a "once-in-a-millennium natural disaster." The Chinese internet users, who usually remain silent, seemed to have a lot to say about this: "How can a country mock the misfortunes of others while not admitting to its own fault?" On the other hand, the president of Taiwan expressed her condolences for this misfortune in Henan Province.

It has long been said that the people of Beijing would clap their hands in joy whenever a significant earthquake hit southern China. As the saying goes, "The misfortunes of others taste like honey." The Japanese government and business corporations must realize that the state-led politics of China and North Korea are far from trustworthy.

This book presents an objective review of the Earth by a savior from outer space. I think that we should accept the content with humility.

Ryuho Okawa
Master & CEO of Happy Science Group
July 23, 2021

Spiritual Messages from Metatron Light in the Times of Crisis

Originally recorded in Japanese on June 18, 2021
at Special Lecture Hall, Happy Science, Japan
and later translated into English.

Metatron

A space being from Planet Include in Sagittarius. A part of Jesus Christ's space soul (Amor). One of the highest-ranking angels (seraphim) who protect the Lord. He is also one of the gods of Light. In the past, when major battles occurred on Earth, he provided support as a symbol of the cosmic power to bring peace to the world on earth. He was once born in Mesopotamia about 6,500 years ago. Currently, he is supporting El Cantare, who has been incarnated on earth as Ryuho Okawa.

1

Asking Metatron about the Various Issues Afflicting the Earth

RYUHO OKAWA

Hello.

The other day, I planned to record spiritual messages from Mr. Metatron, but I didn't manage due to some worldly issues. It feels like a while ago, but now I think it's finally time for a "rematch."

I feel it would be difficult to talk with him if I'm involved in small worldly matters because his message will likely be of a vast scale, so I need to be a little detached from this world.

I know it's challenging to understand Metatron, but at Happy Science, we have already compiled his profile. Some people may laugh about it, but others take it seriously and listen to what he says. Metatron does really exist.

To put it simply, he is a being related to Jesus Christ, but I think we can think of him as someone with a foothold in the universe. It seems that savior-class beings don't just reincarnate on the Earth. They usually have a cosmic soul and often have branch souls that carry out work or undergo training on other planets. So, from their point of view, looking at the Earth may be just like watching a goldfish in a fishbowl.

I have communicated with hundreds of beings that are likely from outer space, but I think the central figures are Yaidron, Metatron, and R. A. Goal. I have come to understand that these three seem to be the most important figures and that no matter how many beings I talk to, that would only cause confusion eventually. So, by listening to what these three beings have to say, I think we can understand how the Earth would look from outer space.

Mr. Metatron, who I'm going to talk to today, is a soul who is related to Jesus. R. A. Goal seems to be a cosmic being related to Shakyamuni Buddha and Yaidron, although he doesn't say it clearly, I guess he is probably related to Moses.

Recalling when Metatron appeared before me, he was present, for example, when I gave a lecture on *Spiritual Messages from Mao Zedong* in Nagoya Shoshinkan (February 11, 2019), where Mr. B, one of today's questioners, was the head minister back then. This occasion was a typical example.

In the early stages of my activities, when I wrote *The Laws of the Sun* and *The Golden Laws* (both published by IRH Press), the diplomatic relations between Japan and China had already been restored. Also, the United States had just restored diplomatic relations with China, and Japan seemed to be on good terms with China and supported China's development through economic cooperation. I thought that Mao Zedong would not be so bad a person and assumed he would be in the fifth-dimensional Realm of the Good. But recent findings have proven that he doesn't possibly belong to that realm.

When I was about to give a lecture on *Spiritual Messages from Mao Zedong* and stayed overnight in a hotel the day before, Mao Zedong's spirit had already found its way to the hotel and attempted to disturb me. At times like this, Mr. Metatron and others come and protect me by setting up a spiritual barrier with their mighty power.

Also, when I gave lectures overseas, for example, when I visited Germany and Taiwan, it seemed that the support from Jesus alone was not enough. Hence, Mr. Metatron also came to double the support.

When I give a lecture that would influence the world, it is necessary to be quite vigilant in all directions because disturbances at an unusual scale may be expected.

He (Metatron) has been sending out various messages concerning the state of the Earth. Some of them seem to be somewhat out of sync with the understanding of people on earth, but he also shows ideas about the near future, so there are things that we can understand. I have already published what he had to say in the form of UFO readings and other books.

Well, it is difficult to make a general statement because there are all sorts of different opinions. Although people do not say (outwardly) that they read the books of Happy Science or listen to what we are expressing, I believe that governments around the world, as well as the Japanese government and mass media, are slowly becoming influenced by the messages Happy Science is putting out and are gradually moving toward accepting our ideas as the norm.

I'm a bit reluctant to ask him too many questions about fleeting matters, but I'd like to hear his opinions from a macroscopic perspective or about issues that are a little hard for humans to make a judgment on. I would be grateful if he could give us his opinions from a slightly different perspective or a disinterested party's viewpoint.

So, let's get started.

Now, we would like to ask for a word from Mr. Metatron, who is from Planet Include in Sagittarius and spiritually related to Jesus Christ.

Mr. Metatron, we would appreciate it if you could give us your thoughts on the various issues currently afflicting Japan and the entire Earth. Thank you.

[*About 10 seconds of silence.*]

2

The Truth about the Coronavirus Pandemic and China's Strategy

What is behind the G7 countries' growing condemnation of China

METATRON

I'm here.

A

Thank you very much for always giving us guidance and blessings. Today, as we have the opportunity to receive your spiritual guidance, we would like to ask you about the various issues affecting the entire world.

METATRON

Good.

A

Since last year, the coronavirus has been spreading all over the world, and the situation continues. May I ask you to tell us what you have to say about the current situation and other issues that concern you the most?

METATRON

The news reports seem to have covered only this issue for about a year and a half now. It may have been the most significant incident in a long time. In the sense that it affected the whole world, it's indeed something that only happens once in a hundred years. It's not just regional, but it affects the entire world, and no one has been able to pinpoint the root cause of it. People are trying to come up with different countermeasures to grope for a solution. This seems to be what's happening now.

My collaborators and I have been consistently saying from the beginning that the leakage from the Wuhan Institute of Virology was the cause. However, in the process of the U.S. presidential election, the forces that were trying to bring down President Trump, namely the leftist forces, spread information contradicting the truth to impede Mr. Trump's anti-China views. For example, they spread theories that said the coronaviruses were spontaneously generated or that their origin couldn't be identified.

Well, China itself was apologizing in the beginning, but then, it began to say, "No, coronavirus might have been mixed in the frozen food from abroad," and made other claims. Then, amid the confusion, the vaccine was created, cities were locked down, emergency measures were taken, and all sorts of fusses were everywhere.

I think it has been about half a year since Mr. Biden became the president, and it seems that his administration is finally getting to the point where they can do things without criticizing Mr. Trump. Their attention seems to be gradually turning to the Wuhan bio lab. I'm sure they knew about it (that the virus originated in China). But they dispersed the (spontaneous generation) theory as a part of the electoral campaign.

Well, even if they had the "answer," they can't say what it is until they decide how to deal with China in the end. Politicians' responsibilities include making various simulations, so I don't think they can only support scientific facts.

At the recent G7 Summit and other conferences, there have been some very harsh comments about China. Some countries that used to be positive about Mr. Xi Jinping's One Belt One Road Initiative, with China entering from

Asia to Europe and creating the Silk Road of the Sea, and other countries that have the highest trade volume with China have started to condemn China's suppression of human rights and other issues. They are now acting in unison.

And the issue behind it is... As a matter of fact, there were ultimately the issues of coronavirus behind it, and before they could address that point, they needed to clarify their attitude toward China. So, I think they are first working on laying the groundwork.

The Japanese government was the only one that did not clearly condemn China until the end of their Diet session, and I've heard that some people are saying this is quite disgraceful. As for other countries, the West agrees on protecting the fundamental values of a modern nation, such as "democratic values," "basic human rights," "rule of law," "separation of powers," and so on. On the other hand, even though Japan is supposed to be a member of the West, for some reason, the Japanese government seems to be maintaining an ambiguous attitude.

The government's attitude is probably due to economic reasons. Japanese corporations do extensive business, with significant investments and many factories and employees in China. There is pressure from the business community, so the government must be thinking about the risks of making hasty political decisions. Well, as long as China is concerned, economic and military issues are so intertwined. I think the Japanese government is avoiding the problem due to the danger of provoking the counterpart before making sufficient preparations.

As for the domestic situation in Japan, no military issues are likely present, so it won't become like Myanmar. Even if the government bans doing business after 7 or 8 p.m. or bans serving alcohol, Japanese people will not violently attack a police station, the Diet building, or the prime minister's residence. The government seems to think it's easy to deal with the domestic situation while international matters involve more risk.

The root cause is, as I mentioned earlier, already apparent, as we have been saying from the beginning. The truth is that the culprit had planned to cause almost no damage by the virus within China but to release it to other foreign countries. However, somehow it leaked out from their laboratory. A few people were infected, which then caused it to spread to the surrounding areas. That resulted in tens of thousands of patients in Wuhan City, which meant a part of their conspiracy was revealed at the early stage.

I think the situation will be uncovered in due course. But if the cause is to be identified, it would be necessary to go as far as preparing for an international conflict. So, I think we have to interpret the words of the politicians in subtle ways.

The crisis that will be brought about by the idea, "vaccination will calm things down"

METATRON

As for the question of how the situation will proceed... The G7 Summit seems to have concluded "doing our best to provide the vaccine this year, supplying it in huge numbers everywhere including the developing countries, and calming things down by next year or so." But it may be premature to draw conclusions, and we think their views are much too optimistic.

B

Talking about being optimistic, the world, including Japan, is in a very "fuzzy" phase of not knowing how to regard this situation. This situation is probably due to the disparity between people's perceptions and the truth. Do you have any thoughts on the outlook at the end of the year, for example, regarding coronavirus?

METATRON

Right now, Japan's Prime Minister Suga[1] and his aids seem to have decided on the total number of vaccine doses and think that administering a million doses a day will cover all the people and calm the situation down. They seem to use this optimistic outlook to rationalize the hosting of the Olympic Games in Tokyo. However, I have to say this is wishful thinking.

Vaccines are being developed worldwide, but the truth is that China is the only country that has been researching this for a long time. It is normal to research vaccines simultaneously as developing biological weapons, and they have been doing this for more than 15 years. Unlike the other countries that only started researching last year, China has already spent much longer researching coronavirus vaccines.

Many countries provide doses of the vaccines they have developed, and the people seem to let their guard down and do away with face masks. But this is not the end of the story. China's ultimate goal is to make sure that the vaccines made in China are the only ones that will work. This is their goal.

So, what will happen then is that China will bring the world to its knees once again with "vaccine diplomacy" alone.

They managed to do this with the large scale of trade values. They can use their money to invest in other heavily indebted countries and take control of them. They could also pose a military threat, but if this virus spreads worldwide and can only be stopped with a vaccine developed by China, we may have no choice but to "bow down to China." They have actually already thought of this option.

B

If that is the case, do you think preparations are already being made to defeat or evade the vaccines that the advanced countries in the West have developed? And will they launch attacks in sequence?

METATRON

Yeah. As I mentioned earlier, there are already over a hundred and several tens of variants, and they already have them in place. And to make it go viral, only one person is enough. If a single person manages to get into a crowd, it's pretty easy to infect a few others, and it will further spread.

B

We have already written an article in *The Liberty* magazine (August 2021 issue). There was a research paper from a few years ago on a simulation to spread the symptomless virus by infiltrating the United States and Taiwan. As you say, I guess all preparations have already taken place.

METATRON

That's right. So, even if it's impossible to intrude into a country, there are still pilots and flight attendants of international airlines. These people will go abroad and get off the plane, right? And they have some time off, don't they? That's when they get infected. Then, when those crews go back to their home countries, the virus will spread. This is what happened in Taiwan recently. Even though they successfully blocked the virus so perfectly, the variants actually came in via the pilots and flight attendants on international flights.

B

Was that a planned attack?

METATRON

Yes, indeed.

They can do it. China is a country where it's possible to inflict personal attacks, or rather assassinate people, so that kind of plot is, of course, possible.

B

They targeted the flight attendants and the pilots, then?

METATRON

That's right. Then, if things go as planned, the passengers on the plane may also be affected, but it's impossible to stop the crews from going abroad. You can see a loophole here.

3
Recognize the True Nature of China

Why did coronavirus suddenly spread in Vietnam?

B

This may be a controversial issue, but recently, there has been a rather unusual trend. Since April, there has been a sudden outbreak in Vietnam.

METATRON

That's right.

B

The pandemic in India was also quite abnormal.

METATRON

Yes, it really was abnormal.

B

We still don't have a lot of evidence except for the cases in Taiwan, but the trend seems to be a bit artificial.

METATRON

That's right.

B

So, it was intentional?

METATRON

Yes, it was intentional.

From China's point of view, Vietnam is a traitor. It was a communist country that fought against the United States as China's "subordinate." During the Vietnam War, Chinese troops fought on a large scale in Vietnam and offered logistic services as part of their seedy deals conducted behind closed doors. The Vietnam War was fought extensively until the U.S. withdrew from the region, and it made the Americans feel very weary of war.

I think that Vietnam probably suffered the damage of two million lives or even more. Among them were Chinese soldiers of the People's Liberation Army who fought alongside the Vietnamese, and many of them were also killed or wounded. So, with a significant sacrifice, China defeated the U.S. and drove them out of South Vietnam, which was under American control.

This was a significant victory for China. It's a secret victory that they can't openly boast about. Although they couldn't take South Korea (in the Korean War), they managed to take Vietnam.

Vietnam, which had been a communist country, started implementing a market economy. While it still would have been acceptable if it were a Chinese-style market economy, it gradually became more and more American-oriented.

Similarly, Kim Jong-un of North Korea received a suggestion from President Trump, saying, "Why don't you become like Vietnam?" Because there would be no future for communism, the former president suggested that Mr. Kim lead North Korea toward an American-style market economy and liberalism. Well, Mr. Kim seems to be affected by that a little because North Korea is starting to change.

Therefore, Vietnam is a traitor to China and is now trying very hard to build a stronger relationship with Japan, to seek support.

Japan has offered vaccines to Vietnam as well as Taiwan and several other countries. But they (the Chinese) intend to create a situation in which vaccines made in the U.S. and Britain will not be effective even if they are distributed from Japan. This is an advantageous situation for China, isn't it?

B

Yes, that's right.

Will the vaccination measures end in a cat-and-mouse game?

B

I found what you said to be very realistic. For example, you touched upon the development of vaccines. Those who are producing vaccines, the American pharmaceutical companies, are somehow connected to the People's Liberation Army to varying degrees. It seems that the Chinese military has information about what kind of vaccines are being developed in advance.

Then, of course, it is certainly easy to assume there will be a virus that beats those vaccines.

This is one of the problems that the world probably doesn't know.

Another problem is that China seems to have collected in advance more than a thousand strains of coronaviruses. Those will serve as a foundation for future variants, and they seem to be thinking of launching these variants one after another, cutting and pasting them as they see fit...

METATRON

Yes, I see that.

B

If that's the case, it seems to me that no matter how many vaccines we produce in the future, there can be something that beats them, and maybe that is already on their list at this stage. What is your view on this?

METATRON

As you know, it takes at least a year to develop a vaccine, and the clinical tests have not yet been completed. In short, without a follow-up study to see if the vaccine is effective, we can't really know if it's working or not. So, there will inevitably be a time lag of, well, at least a year.

If different variants come out in the meantime, there's no way to confront them in time. You will have no way of dealing with them.

So, if Britain or Israel proceeded with the vaccination process and people started taking their face masks off, China may say, "Well, let's put in a different kind," then people will have to put on their face masks again.

B

Yes, that's right. British people will start wearing masks in a hurry again, I guess.

METATRON

That's the consequence. So, if the (British) aircraft carrier and its fleet approach off the coast of Hong Kong, the virus will probably spread in Britain again.

B

I see.

METATRON

This will have to happen.

You see, no country can prevent the spreading of viruses via people because it's impossible to burn them all with a flamethrower.

B

Then, basically, we have to assume that the vaccination measures will not work?

METATRON

Well, it's like a cat-and-mouse game, isn't it?

No, it can work in some cases. It does work if you completely swallow what China demands. They'll stop the spreading at that stage. They will say, "Well, now that we're on friendly terms with you, we won't cause harm anymore."

It's like when a heel wrestler does something terrible out of the referee's eyeshot. Although he is doing bad things and throwing out a hint, he never leaves a clue. Like such a villain, some people are working really hard on such a kind of plot in this world.

This situation is quite inconceivable in an open and transparent society, but there are countries where such things can be done without hesitation or shame. Well, about 2,000 years ago, there were many such cases. This is also happening now.

A state that resembles a giant Aum cult has emerged

B

In that case, as China's research on vaccines is 15 years ahead of the rest of the world, and with the vaccines in hand, they are applying a kind of "vaccine diplomacy" to bring other countries to their knees by saying, "If you want to be cured, do as we say..."

METATRON

Yes. That's right.

You can get a sense of what is happening. When you somehow find out that the heel wrestler pulls out a weapon beyond the referee's eyeshot and hits the back of the opponent's head, then you can imagine what the heel would say: "If you don't want to be hit, then do as I say." Such as, "Go down on the seventh." Well, just like that.

C

Huh. Such "arrangements" are gradually becoming more and more...

METATRON

Yes, they are taking shape behind the scenes.

C

Behind the scenes?

METATRON

Yes, these things never surface and are done hidden behind locked doors.

C

In that case, if they want to save their people's lives, some countries will likely have no choice but to surrender. I'm afraid they will have to take part in the hoax, the dark strategy China is orchestrating behind the scenes.

METATRON

That's right.

You see, in Japan, some 26 years ago, the Aum cult group produced poisonous gas and biological weapons. But if you look at the scale of the nation of China, it is tens of thousands or even hundreds of thousands of times bigger than that cult. If hundreds of thousands of the Aum cult emerge and attack you, there will be nothing you can do about it.

You can imagine in that way. You may think such a thing can't possibly happen, but in a nation that does not recognize fundamental human rights, only the nation's sovereignty exists.

Only the state as a person owns its personality, and the people have no fundamental human rights. The priority is to protect the nation's dignity, supremacy, honor, and desire for power. That's why they regard the crime of treason as more serious than any other crime.

You can see this happening in Hong Kong. The anti-Beijing newspaper publisher has already been subjected to the "final extinction" strategy. The owner will be arrested, and all his personal assets, as well as the assets of the company, have been frozen. He can't even publish a newspaper without money, right? (The newspaper discontinued its business in July.)

Chinese authorities think they can do anything based on their domestic laws. If it serves their primary purpose to protect the nation, develop it, and drive away foreign countries, they think they can do anything they want.

Chinese history tells us all about this. It's all about the survival of the country itself. The state itself has been a kind of living creature, like behemoth or leviathan in the Western context.

What is China's strategy to break the anti-China coalition?

B

If that is the case, I wonder how we should respond to the nation and groups with such behavioral patterns and strategies...

METATRON

Well, I'm sure China does expect opposition but just thinks, "The opponents will fall over halfway, back away, and never go the full distance. They may impose some economic sanction or a censure resolution, but if the actual war starts, most of the countries would be frightened and think that there would be no benefit in opposing us, and they will retreat."

Even if Britain sends an aircraft carrier and Germany sends a warship to Asia, which rarely happens, China will probably try to demonstrate that it is not a threat of any kind.

Australia is a small country, and it used to be pro-China, but now it is anti-China, having realized China's strategy for military hegemony and acquiring natural resources. From China's point of view, Australia is a pain in the neck, so China is imposing sanctions.

In short, if there are countries that have taken an anti-China stance, China will choose the small subordinate countries rather than the big ones as prey and bully them brutally. They will beat the weakest countries first.

Then, toward Japan, where people are indecisive and can go either way, China will put pressure, using its economic power and make them care about calculating the profits and losses. In this way, they will break down the solidarity of the coalition of the nations.

Last year, the Democrats and journalists in the States tried hard to blame Mr. Trump for dividing the world. Now that Mr. Biden is in office, the G7 countries and the West are trying to come together and agree on shared values. They are advocating a confrontation with the tyranny of China.

On the other hand, China is trying to hit back with two key phrases, "division" and "interference in the internal affairs." They say they are fighting against foreign powers that attempt to divide the nation and interfere in domestic affairs.

I don't think it will be so easy to overcome this situation.

B

As Master Okawa said at the beginning, even so, what we have been sending out from Happy Science, or rather from Master Okawa, seems to have been influencing the world to a certain extent. In the last few days, all the major Japanese newspapers evaluated the outcome of the G7 Summit and the subsequent meeting between the U.S. and Russia in Geneva. The Japanese media seem to have formed a consensus by saying, "Stop the confrontation between the two-front (China and Russia) and don't get caught in the other side's strategy to divide us." I think we can see our influence here...

METATRON

Ah, I'm afraid that Mr. Biden is a bit too slow. It has been evident since last year.

To win the presidential election, he conspired to attack Russia, blaming Mr. Trump's army of supporters. "By attacking his possible connection to Russia, Trump will fall," he thought and concentrated on attacking Russia.

But in the end, even though Mr. Biden was on good terms with China, now he has to view China as an enemy. If the United States has to fight both countries, even if it teams up with the G7, it will be in a lot of trouble, and the result will be a divided world. Well, that's what's happening, isn't it?

They (China) are trying to work with Iran and are actually thinking of absorbing both North Korea and South Korea altogether. I think they are thinking of taking in Japan as well.

They aim to divide the world into two groups, just like at the time of World War II when the nations were divided into the Axis and the Allied that opposed one another. And before instigating a "hot war," China wants the opponent countries to back away out of fear and collapse as if an army of sheep falls apart.

China knows all about the weaknesses of democracies

B

Talking about America, as you say, Mr. Biden is probably not thinking seriously about anything. But his subordinates seem to be working hard to distract him from the fight against Russia and instead are trying to set the stage so that he can concentrate on the issues with China. There seems to be such an atmosphere around him.

I think we are getting to that point, though.

METATRON

Right.

B

As you mentioned at the beginning, the origin of coronavirus, for example, is definitely known. Still, at the stage of making it public, it will be necessary to decide on the final policy. It takes decisiveness, wouldn't you think?

METATRON

Yes.

B

I'm sure the United States will show its findings to a certain extent and make some announcements about them. What do you think about the chance of the U.S. reaching the point of decision-making or making some kind of judgment?

METATRON

Well, China knows all about the weaknesses of democratic nations, right?

When there are more damages, more losses, or more failures, the approval ratings drop, and then the opposition rises. They know about this very well.

You won't see this consequence in China. There is no such thing as public opinion. It's just a question of how brainwashed people are. The degree of brainwashing is the same as their "public opinion." If the level of brainwashing goes up to 100%, the support rate will be 100%; if the level of brainwashing is more than 90%, the support will be more than 90%. If someone is rebellious against the government and crosses the line, then they'll be just wiped out from this world. It's as simple as that.

4

Japan's Moves Hold the Key to the World

Don't repeat Europe's response at the time of Hitler's emergence

METATRON

What I want you to study now, really, is the atmosphere in Europe when Hitler made his appearance.

At first, people didn't expect that Hitler would go as far as he did. It was admirable and honorable that he managed to rebuild a country that had been torn apart by World War I and to have developed its economy that far. But no one could expect him to start invading other countries so soon, in less than 20 years after the war, so the European countries adopted an appeasement policy.

That resulted in the German invasion of Poland, followed by other consequences. When Germany invaded Poland, people thought it was inevitable as coal, iron, and other natural resources were necessary. Germany promised that it wouldn't go beyond Poland. Toward the Soviet Union, Hitler proposed an alliance to share Poland with Germany.

It was hard to believe that such a downright evil person was elected to head a nation. That was inconceivable. But I have to say that this is the nature of those in power.

That was a historical fact in Germany. But if you look at the history of China, those in power have all been like this. Only exceptionally, a few virtuous monarchs appeared, but there have only been tyrants in most times. The stronger, the more invasive, and the more victorious against the enemies, the more they have been respected.

So, from the perspective of China's history, although you are now criticizing them, saying, "They are invading Tibet," "They are invading Uyghur," or "They are also invading Mongolia," they would say, "What are you talking about? In the history of China, there have been many ages when we have been occupied and taken by them. We have been fighting against one another throughout history, and the stronger side wins." This is their idea.

The Uyghurs were probably the enemies of the Han Chinese in the past, such as the Xiongnu. They were so intimidating that the Han Chinese were forced to build the Great Wall of China. They even made the Great Wall of China for protection against such people, but now that they're inside Chinese territory, it's only natural that they will be sinicized and brainwashed. This is how the Chinese think.

They are criticized for violating fundamental human rights, but in their eyes, these people are barbarians. Because they are foreign barbarians, China's assimilation policy is an absolute good. That's what the Chinese think, but this line of thought isn't generally understood.

B

I think it is crucial to expose the true nature of China outright, or rather, to let the world and the Japanese people know about it.

METATRON

I don't know if Japan can expose the truth, but I'm sure Happy Science is not afraid to do so.

Some other people are independent-minded and express their opinions on their own responsibility. Still, they are a bit reluctant to express their views on behalf of the organization they belong to.

B

Recently, I met with a journalist from a major Japanese newspaper who said to me, "Actually, I also believe that the coronavirus is a Chinese biological weapon." Still, he also said, "But I'm sorry, I can't go that far because of company policy."

METATRON

That's natural.

B

Indeed. After all, that's what he said.

METATRON

They (China) have such a foul mouth. Usually, you would think that if you say something bad, it will hurt the other person, or if you say something based on false information, it will hurt your conscience. This is how people feel in normal countries.

However, for people of a country where there is no God, no Buddha, no spiritual world, and no hell, as long as they can fulfill their worldly interests, or what is advantageous to them in this world, that is the "absolute good." They don't care about anything else.

As long as it's something advantageous for them, they will do whatever they want. That is their national character. Because of this difference in mentality, they can say anything they want, even if it goes against the truth.

On the other hand, if you are Japanese, you're likely to be quiet or reserved about expressing opinions against them.

Let's take an example. When Happy Science formed a political party in Japan, the major newspapers and TV stations would not cover it. They would completely censor the information so that it wouldn't influence floating voters. These kinds of things are done silently, without saying anything about that explicitly.

If (hypothetically) Happy Science were a "pawn" of the Chinese government, what would you say? You would say all kinds of nasty things. You would keep saying bad things about TV stations and their newspapers and other media. You would thoroughly beat up on anything that doesn't benefit you or is harmful to you. That's what they (Chinese) would do in real life.

The question is whether this kind of mentality should be tolerated. If you include the 1.4 billion people in China, overseas Chinese, and others scattered overseas, there are about 2 billion people of Chinese descent. This is a significant share of the global population, and we can't get rid of them. If you were to accept their mentality to think, "It is more advantageous to claim our own interests only," then the values of this world, for example, Christian values and Buddhist values, would all be overturned, wouldn't they?

If you believe in the teachings of altruism and think, "We should do our best for others even at the cost of our patience," it would sound to them like an underdog mentality. For them, it's the mentality of antelopes or sheep. They can become easy prey for wolves. All they have to do is to attack the weakest ones first.

Who are the "key players" in putting China under siege?

C

Earlier, you said that we couldn't announce that China is the source of the coronavirus unless we envision preparing for international conflicts and decide how to deal with China in the future.

One of my colleagues mentioned this, but I would like to ask you about the future from the perspective of decision making as seen from a global perspective. Mr. Metatron, from your point of view, from the perspective of the universe, what should the decision on Earth, particularly toward China, be?

METATRON

I think the key player is Japan.

C

Really? The key player is Japan?

METATRON

That's right. It's Japan. If Japan makes a clear decision to adopt the Western values of the G7 countries, China will be besieged.

C

If Japan makes a decision...

METATRON

Only if it decides. And in terms of relations with Russia, you should prioritize building a siege around China even if you have to shelve the issues of the Northern Territories. Most of the islands have only fishing and marine products. You can't get profit except for kelp and fish, and the value would be no more than a few hundred million yen. Maybe, there are family tombs as well, but that's about it.

Therefore, China will be ruined if Japan can disregard the minor points, put things in perspective, and decide on those two main points.

C

That means the first point is to decide on adopting the Western value system upheld by the G7 countries. And in terms of relations with Russia, we should prioritize building a siege around China even if we have to shelve the issues of the Northern Territories. That's how to look at the situation from the universe.

METATRON

That's right. Yes, you have to take these actions.

The rest of the group nations will join forces. But how about Japan which is the closest to China?

A similar situation took place a little more than 100 years ago, or 120 years ago. It was the time when China was in a miserable condition. After the Opium War, China was occupied by many countries, and many civil wars broke out. The problem was so bad that the West asked Japan to send troops to guard and protect China like a police force. Consequently, Japanese troops were stationed in China to put the situation under control. The current situation is the same as the situation 120 years ago.

So, if Japan can be relied on, the monolithic stance of the West will not be broken. But if Japan, out of concern for its own interests, offers a helping hand to China because it has to protect UNIQLO, for example, or asks the new Emperor and Empress to officially visit China because the coronaviruses seem to be subdued in China whereas other countries are still risky, it will be the repetition of what happened after the Tiananmen Square incident all over again.

B

Indeed. Incidentally, the next issue of *The Liberty* magazine will be sending out a message that will be a severe blow to China, including the problems of UNIQLO. Japan is currently taking an ambiguous stance without considering justice and is being hindered by its own economic interests in China. Our message will be, "Japan, show your flag, make it clear to the West, and persuade them, then the situation will improve."

METATRON

Japan's attitude toward Myanmar is the same as that toward China, isn't it? Regarding the military regime in Myanmar, the Japanese government cannot state whether it thinks the regime is good or not, can it? It keeps an indecisive attitude. The problem is that there are Japanese citizens and factories over there.

From China's point of view, they don't want factories to be moved out of China and transferred to other Asian countries. Therefore, they need to spread the viruses in these countries. Then the Japanese businesses would say, "Oh, the viruses are also spreading there, then it's difficult to transfer our factories and Japanese employees from China and start manufacturing in those countries."

What was the opinion of the guardian spirit of Prime Minister Suga, who visited Ryuho Okawa?

B

At a rather casual, almost off-the-record press conference after the G7 Summit, Mr. Suga said, "No, we are not going to build a siege on China."

METATRON

[*Chuckles.*]

B

He was talking to a foreign journalist, so I thought, "At the very least, don't say things like that!"

METATRON

Well, he is a "Machiavellist," isn't he? I can't tell what he really means. He may not be telling the truth. Having said that, he may be willing to do that, and it's hard to know.

He is the first Japanese prime minister to claim himself as a Machiavellist, so it's difficult to know what he was really thinking behind the scenes.

At least, he (the guardian spirit of Mr. Suga) came to Master Okawa at night after a no-confidence motion was submitted against his cabinet.

B

Oh, really?

METATRON

Yeah, but that wasn't recorded. Mrs. Okawa decided not to record Mr. Suga's (guardian spirit's) message because she thought it would be trivial anyway. She just talked with him briefly, and that was it. I'm very sorry there wasn't enough of a story to go to print for *The Liberty* magazine.

B

Not at all.

METATRON

We were watching this.

Anyway, Mr. Suga's guardian spirit was complaining, "There have been some sharp opinions from Happy Science, but many of them are in favor of the opposition."

He said, "The opposition parties have forged a bipartisan coalition, and say things like 'It's necessary to lower the consumption tax to 5%,' or 'The Olympic Games should be canceled or postponed.'" He also complained, "Other things opposition parties are saying seem to be close to what Happy Science has to say."

He wanted to negotiate, "Why wouldn't you say things like, 'I'm for the Tokyo Olympic Games!' 'Vaccinations should be promoted further. So, let's get people to accept vaccines!' or 'It's not necessary to lower the consumption tax anymore.'" He complained, "What you (Happy Science) are saying is similar to the opposition parties."

However, the information wasn't offered to *The Liberty* magazine because it hardly counts as news.

B

No, it's not worth it. It seems to me that he (P.M. Suga) has brought this situation onto himself because everything he has done works in favor of the opposition.

Why does Prime Minister Suga want to push forward with the Tokyo Olympic Games?

B

Now that we have touched upon the domestic matters of Japan, I would like to ask you about them further.

You have just given us a bird's-eye view of where the world's problems are. Actually, when you gave a brief talk about a month ago, I believe it was about the domestic political situation, and you made a few comments such as, "You will be entering into a kind of political vacuum, and the situation will be rather risky." It seems that Mr. Suga is going to charge ahead with a single-minded focus on the Olympic Games. I would appreciate it if you could tell us what you think will happen in Japan, or what you think should be done.

METATRON

As a politician, he seems to be thinking, "Life is too short" or rather, "If the life of the administration is going to be short anyway, I want at least my name to be remembered." It would be a true feeling of a politician.

"We decided to go ahead with the Olympics under such difficult circumstances, and the Tokyo Olympic Games were held in 2021. The prime minister at that time was Mr. Suga," in this way, he wants to leave his mark on history.

Also, if the Children's Agency and the Digital Agency are established during his term as prime minister, such achievements will be included in Japanese history textbooks. Probably that's all he wants to do, and what happens afterward would be of no concern to him.

He hopes that everything goes well and creates a virtuous cycle. His wishful scenario would be: "As a result of offering a million doses of the vaccine every day, the coronaviruses will be brought under control very quickly, there will be no problem hosting the Olympic Games, and the economy will recover. Then, all will be due to the excellent decision of the prime minister, and he might even be praised for being as decisive as Winston Churchill. There might be a possibility for him to serve as prime minister for a few more years." Well, it's a gamble.

He is unsure how many more years he can serve, but if he has to quit in September, he would rather want to leave his name in history.[1]

The fifth coronavirus wave and how it may affect the Winter Olympic Games in China

B

Indeed. According to a simulation, if things continue as they are now, the peak of the fifth coronavirus wave that Master Ryuho Okawa mentioned will come in late August, around the beginning of the Paralympic Games. So, the games for athletes with physical disabilities will start amid a very difficult situation. Then, in the first week of September, after the Games, the prime minister seems to be undergoing the worst-case scenario that it's not clear whether or not the House of Representatives is dissolved.[2]

METATRON

Well, it's just a matter of making political broadcasts from the basement, as Mr. Biden demonstrated in the United States last year (2020). Doing this is not impossible, although giving street speeches may be difficult.

As for China, they surely want to hold the Winter Olympic Games in February next year. Now, there is a possibility for them to hold the Games because China claims almost no increase in the number of patients, so there is nothing to stop them. Therefore, they are currently saying "yes" to the Olympics in Japan.

In this relationship, if Japan takes a defiant attitude toward China, there may be a fifth wave, hmm...

The fifth wave means if the Chinese team brings "something," that will do the trick.

B

Yes, it's possible.

METATRON

There is no telling whether they are bringing viruses with them, so they can bring them in. Many athletes are coming to Japan, so if they leave the viruses in Japan, that's it. They will spread.

However, it's not desirable to implement the plan during the Olympic Games in Tokyo if it destroys the Games, so they are currently working on detailed calculations.

Whether the fifth wave will happen or not, that still depends on the global situation.

B

I understand.

5

Observing the Current Political Situation in Japan

Will we see the return of the year 2009 when the ruling party lost in a landslide?

B

Actually, I was thinking about the feature articles in the next issue of *The Liberty* magazine and what we should emphasize. From the viewpoint of Happy Science, Mr. Suga seems to have always made wrong moves, so we have no choice but to advocate things that the opposition parties are likely to follow suit.

Because of such irony, if we were to take a clear stance and advocate, "This is the way things should be," then we would be in trouble if the ruling LDP is defeated miserably. I don't want this to happen as if it were the return of the election in 2009. I wonder how we should look at the political situation in Japan.

METATRON

If the LDP coalition is sorely defeated, then there is a possibility that the Japanese Communist Party will be able to appoint a minister for the first time. Some of its policies are already reflected in the opposition coalition. That's the tricky part, isn't it? Hmm...

I wonder. Well, I guess they will probably gather different parties' seats and work it out in the end.

Also, there is still some uncertainty about the move of Ms. Koike, the governor of Tokyo, you know? If the government appears to be evasive and indecisive, I think she is observing the situation to decide the best timing to take some action.

If that is the case, a political party can possibly be created by the governor of Tokyo. This kind of negotiation may be going on. It's not impossible to make an alternative to the Osaka-based Japan Restoration Party and form a Tokyo-based group. If the media supports it, it could happen in no time at all.

Hmm... Well, you don't want the LDP to lose, but you don't want it to win, either [*laughs*]. This kind of situation is what the media enjoys the most. It's an excellent opportunity for them to wield the power of speech. If it's a close race and it's difficult to predict which side will win or lose, the power of the press will be very effective, and the politicians will have to please the media.

The situation is the same in the United States. The media don't want a ruling party that is too strong. The ideal situation for the media is when the results can turn out to be either way. Then, they can use the power of speech most effectively.

There must be various calculations going on in that context. But well, it seems that some Japanese newspapers are recommending the cancellation of the Olympic Games. Much of the public opinion is also against the Games. Well, NHK doesn't seem to be opposing it, though.

Well, the question of whether the media will take it to that level and take a totally confrontational stance, hmm... and whether what happened in 2009 will really happen again. Happy Science seems to be caught in a state of immobility with these regards, right?

Well, a temporary collapse may be unavoidable. Although there are not particularly good alternatives, hmm... what can I say, we need to get the politicians to take responsibility. What is happening now is that, in a sense, all of the things the Abe Administration tried to do during his term are now going down the drain.

B
Yes, that's right.

METATRON
Isn't that? He was trying to boost the economy by bringing in lots of foreign tourists, especially Chinese. Also, he supplied ample funds to raise stock prices to the extent that inflation does not occur. He created new ministries and agencies to negotiate with the liberals on various subjects. I think what Mr. Abe did is backfiring on the current administration.

Happy Science must be a kind of threat for them. Prime Minister Suga, or his guardian spirit, doesn't like the idea that the opposition might gain a little more power, as it may be possible this time. He is probably afraid that if Happy Science decides to support the opposition, the balance is lost. Consequently, the ruling party will lose seats and lose the majority...

B

I see.

METATRON

I guess that is what he's thinking.

Japan's "socialist policies" have made it impossible to distinguish between the ruling party and the opposition parties

C

May I ask you about an economic issue?

Under current circumstances, we are in the midst of the recession caused by the coronaviruses, and quite a few companies have gone under and are in trouble. Despite all kinds of grants, subsidies, and so on, it is becoming hard to see the future.

Master Ryuho Okawa gave a lecture entitled "How to Fight Against the Recession Caused by Coronavirus." He predicted that this recession would not end as a minor cyclical adjustment lasting for two or three years.

He also pointed out that although Japan is not a communist country, the government and local governments are declaring a state of emergency to pause all activities of specific industry sectors. He has given some cautionary remarks such as "Japan seems to be preparing to become like North Korea."

Master also pointed out that the central figures of the United States are also becoming tainted with communism and are choosing the policies to spread the money out of exploited wealth.

In his lecture, Master Okawa suggested developing a resilient character and keeping going with perseverance. He indicated that a consumption-led economy alone will not be powerful enough to bring about recovery and that it will be difficult to expect a pickup for a while. He also suggested we work to gain resilience and create value, and what we should do now is to "create."

He also told us that we are currently experiencing "economics of distrust" where people look at each other as a kind of germ, so we need to create new "economics of trust" that requires us to establish faith firmly.

Now, Japan seems to be immersed in the "economics of distrust" and influenced by communist ideologies and even attempting to become like North Korea. The same situation is present in the United States. How would you observe the circumstances, from the cosmic perspective, in light of the history of the Earth?

METATRON

From my point of view, the government is not necessarily conservative or right-wing. Instead, it is adopting more and more socialist policies, so it looks as if there is no need for the opposition parties to exist.

For example, look at the government's decision yesterday (June 17, 2021); it includes something like "The suspension of business will remain in place for restaurants that serve alcoholic beverages after 7 p.m." You see, this kind of thing has never been possible except for the times of rationing right after the war.

B

Yes, it's almost like marshal law.

METATRON

That's right. This kind of government decision usually leads to an uprising. However, Japanese people have been tamed over the past year to accept the current situation as normal. And before that, during Mr. Abe's term, there were times when air alert sirens went off, and people were warned to take cover against North Korean missiles. In a way, Japan has an affinity to national socialism.

So, you are already in a situation where you cannot distinguish between ruling and opposition parties [*laughs*]. Even if the opposition parties come up with specific policies, the ruling party immediately takes them in. Well, I think the "age of chaos" is about to begin, and it will be hard to distinguish between the two.

The ruling coalition is already set to win votes with subsidies. This attitude is no different from what the communist party and other opposition parties are advocating. Komeito, the coalition partner, has policies no different from the opposition. It is all about spreading the money around, for example, giving 100,000 yen for a newborn baby. The politicians are bribing the population on a national scale.

Moreover, in an attempt to distribute subsidies, they want to create the Digital Agency to put all people's data under control. In the end, the authorities want to know where each person is and what they are doing, as well as the movement of all kinds of assets and money.

Well, cash may become less and less handy, and with digital money, it will be possible to know immediately who bought what and where. In addition, with the increasing number of surveillance cameras in place, it will be possible to crack down on all kinds of criminal acts.

From China's point of view, it would be impossible for a criminal to rob a police box and escape with a gun for a week like it is in Japan. There are already cameras everywhere in China, so it's easy for the criminal to get spotted. In a sense, Japan is obviously aiming to be sinicized.

Put various thoughts in perspective for Japan, which is in the process of sinicization

METATRON

If the state or the government aims to make itself become like China, then there is not much difference from the opposition's stance. It means that they are only different in name.

The term "liberal democracy" is just a pretext for the ruling Liberal Democratic Party. It's not democracy, but they are taking a government-first policy. The government wants to lead everything and restricts freedom. Now they are trying to take all the liberty away and create a surveillance society. They aim to bring about an ultimately "government-led" surveillance society.

Besides, the Children's Agency is virtually aiming at birth control, which is similar to China. The state decides on the one-child policy, the two-child policy, or the three-child policy. There is no freedom, is there? I think Japan is getting closer to this kind of country.

There is talk of criticizing UNIQLO, but the country itself may be becoming closer to China. In a way, it seems that Japan is moving toward making itself a province of China.

On the other hand, if the United States starts taking measures to win the votes of blacks and immigrants, the left will gain a much stronger position.

As for what can happen after that, the era that started after the Industrial Revolution will end after experiencing a certain level of prosperity. After the end of a period, the question of what comes next has not yet been decided.

Rather, humanity has not yet made a decision. It may be your job to draw a picture, though.

The trend of modernization that has occurred since the Industrial Revolution, since the 18th century, may possibly be coming to an end. So, it's about "how to picture the world after that," isn't it?

Japan has been lagging far behind, so you need to consider gaining ground again. "The race for colonies" on a cosmic scale has already begun. So, I know it is very difficult to take the lead in fundamental thoughts from this point on.

However, it might be better not to get caught up in the conventional way of thinking, but instead, put various thoughts in perspective from the standpoint of what is the right thing to do. Otherwise, it won't work.

6

The Current State of the Earth as Seen from the Cosmic Perspective

How to confront the forces that are developing hell via China

A

You briefly touched upon the cosmic perspective. Looking back the last year (2020) and this year, it was Master Ryuho Okawa who gave the most accurate insight into the situation of the whole world.

Recent spiritual readings suggest that this is not just about a global virus war but that there may be an intervention from outer space. Also, we understand that there may be involvement from the "flip-side universe." Could you please tell us something about the actual situation?

METATRON

As far as viruses are concerned, there are quite a few strains that China has gathered and created on its own. If the viruses can be blocked with vaccines or other measures, then they would say, "There are still a variety of viruses in outer space, so we may expect the supply from out there."

If there are attempts to destroy China, they will launch a wave of assaults against the opposing countries and cause misfortune.

To put it bluntly, this is because there are some opposing forces in our society, well, from outer space, as to what should be done to change the Earth. There are actually forces that are aiming at world hegemony using China.

Well, we have fought and won against them many times in the past. But if the Earth becomes a magnetic field that is compatible with the opposing forces, then the countries, or rather the planet, will no longer be a place we can influence with our values. Then, those who have matching wavelengths will be able to live on planet Earth. Consequently, such souls will be able to immigrate.

I think Confucius once said in his spiritual messages, "China is now an extremely totalitarian country. The 1.4 billion people of China are like a school of fish that are pulled by a trawler. When they go up to heaven, everyone goes up, and when they go down to hell, everyone goes down." I think he is right.

C

The whole of 1.4 billion will surely go to hell, I guess.

METATRON

Indeed, the whole of them to hell. But if the population of the other side increases, then the realm will become the "heaven"... or rather, it will become a paradise for the villains. You know, there are lots of cities like that, controlled by the *yakuza*, the mafia. There could be a city controlled by gangs and another city controlled by criminals. For them, it's heaven, and if they want to expand their territories, they will.

I forgot to mention this earlier, but Mr. Abe wanted to attract foreign tourists and build casinos. He aimed to attract them and make them spend money. But the current trend of closing down the nightlife districts is apparently going against such intentions.

If the government keeps sending out "No to Alcohol" messages like now, it's natural for people to become allergic to it. So, I'm sure they will try to do the opposite this time.

In any case, there is a high possibility for the world to become a place where everything done with Chinese capital is OK, while everything else will be regarded as taboos. So, the "Japanese decision" is extremely weighty.

As Master Okawa said, both Australia and Taiwan are moving toward protecting their own values. Germany is also moving in the direction of protecting theirs, as well as Britain and Canada. So now, we are at a crossroads of whether this Anglo-American value system continues to be the leading one in the next century onward.

Therefore, the messages from Happy Science should be sent out with this in mind, and you should present the future of society. Regardless of whether the ruling party or the opposition seizes power, you should tell the administration, "This is the future," and "This is how things should unfold." They shouldn't just concentrate on matters that would affect who wins or loses based on the number of votes. So, I think it is crucial to educate the mass media.

Don't stick too much to conventional ideas that are rigid in ideology. Well, in the end, there was no difference between Hitler's national socialism and what Stalin did in the Soviet Union. The right and the left were similar. In a totalitarian state, what the ruler does is the same, that is, hell is just unfolding.

It's your job to stop hell from expanding. Yes.

A

It means that a pathway from the flip-side universe has been created on the Earth.

METATRON

That's done. Yes.

A

Meaning that a "black hole" is being created?

METATRON

Well, but we definitely intend to win, though.

Why Japan's space mission lags far behind

A

We had a bit of news last month that China has started Mars exploration. It's said to be the second only to the United States. I'm afraid that forces with bad intentions are ahead of us, and Japan lags far behind. Could you tell us something about the direction of humanity's relationship with outer space?

METATRON

(In Japan) military affairs are too restricted in many ways. The academic community tries to avoid anything that could lead to military research and uses the power word "peace" to restrain Japan.

Think about police activities at the domestic level. If such a rogue nation appears on a global level, it's quite natural to deter aggression by the joint defense of those countries with the same values. I believe that the time has come for Japan to destroy the common beliefs of the postwar era.

I think the time has come for the common belief formed in the post-war era to be destroyed. So, I hope you work hard on this.

The question is, "What would you do if you were back to square one and had to start over with a clean slate?" You must do what you think has to be done.

For example, South Korea is openly conducting defense drills on Takeshima, which you claim to be Japanese territory. They are using their army to do defense training. But Japan is just verbally protesting and doing nothing.

Besides, although the Japanese government says the Senkaku Islands are Japanese territory, China invariably claims the islands are its core interest. However, Japan doesn't even conduct military training to defend the Senkaku Islands.

I wonder about Japan's attitude. It's a bit awkward for us to say this, but I think this situation can be described with a saying, "Those who do not enforce their rights will not be protected," in the legal context. Even though there are laws... There are laws to protect people, countries, and companies, but indeed, those who do not enforce their rights will not be protected, right?

For example, if a burglar breaks in, there are laws to catch the burglar. But if a burglar steals from you, and you think, “That can’t be helped. No, we can’t do anything about that, so it’s OK. I don’t like violence,” then there’s no way of catching the burglar.

If the results are like that, the burglars will get a taste of success and will likely break into various houses night after night... Well, if burglars break into houses and take people’s property, then it will be a “bad country.” A time will come when Batman, Superman, and many other heroes have to appear, so to speak.

I think you need to have a firm grasp of the concept “Those who do not enforce their rights will not be protected” once again. It would be extremely difficult for a country that does not seem to know whether it has national sovereignty to compete against the country that audaciously highlights its own national sovereignty.

B

I intend to touch upon this topic in *The Liberty* magazine because I expect Mr. Suga will handle the situation in his Machiavellian way if he gets our messages. I'm sure he is willing to fight, to some extent, as far as this situation is concerned.

METATRON

Yes. Well, even though they don't seem to be listening to the information from Happy Science, I see them gathering all the information they can. Having gathered information, they carefully read and assess the content of *The Liberty* and other sources. Well, they seem to be thinking about what to do as they gather information and see what Happy Science has to say.

It's not only about the seats of the Diet. Your opinions are noted. Or else, some conservatives seem to be trying to whip up Happy Science and instigate you to act radically like Yukio Mishima (Japanese novelist and right-wing political activist, 1925-1970) because they think that the government is not reliable anymore.

The situation in the Middle East and the future of the "decarbonized society"

A

I think that Mr. Suga and other people in the administration are referring to the blueprint of the world indicated by Master Ryuho Okawa.

Since the beginning of this year, the situation in the Middle East has been a bit volatile. Recently, in Israel, Mr. Netanyahu stepped down.

METATRON

That's right.

A

In Iran, with the presidential election, there is also a shake-up, which means that anti-American, hardline, ultra-conservative Islamists are likely to win. As for the challenges of the 21st century, I think the issue of Islam is one of them. Could you share your views on these topics with us?

METATRON

Well... If Iran tries to protect itself, it will be against American attacks. Also, an alliance with China for defense has been anticipated.

Iran may change its mind if you show that China is gradually weakening as it is besieged. Iran is unlikely to make its own independent decisions.

However, if you look at the current trends in the world, you are moving toward an era when you cannot use either coal or gas. Well, such thoughts seem to be positively accepted, although I don't necessarily agree.

And then, from Iran's standpoint, you know, they won't be able to sell oil at all. They will have no choice but to create a new industry, building up industries like other ordinary countries.

The Chinese, you know, buy a large amount of natural resources from Iran in secret and use them. China has absolutely no intention of abiding by international treaties from the beginning. Their National Bureau of Statistics will issue false reports, and that's it. Iran probably thinks that China will continue to use oil and coal until the end, therefore China can be relied upon for the time being.

I must point out that even within the Western values, there are some radical ideas like that of Greta from Sweden. It's a different kind of communism centered around environmentalism.

Communism is actually mutating. There are a lot of unusual variants, so I think we have to be careful.

I think Japan is no exception. From your point of view, what Mr. Suga is saying must sound nonsensical in many respects. For example, he is saying that Japan will achieve a fully carbon-neutral society by 2050. But this is as if he is asking for trouble.

Will the royal family and the imperial family be able to survive?

METATRON

If you don't properly claim national sovereignty and change the way you think about the Constitution, you will be in serious trouble in due course.

Article 9 (of the Constitution of Japan) is much disputed, and the media is very harsh on the imperial family system. They have harsh opinions, indeed.

In the background is the decline of religion and also ideas denying the history of Japan. There are definitely leftist ideas.

Well, from the global perspective, royal or imperial families are undoubtedly on the decline. In Britain and Thailand alike, the royal family is in danger. I'm sure they are among the "endangered species."

On the other hand, the prestige of Japanese politicians is incredibly low, and this is quite troublesome. I don't think it's desirable to invite trends to undermine people's faith all at once.

It's true that in countries with a royal family or imperial family, it is not so easy to instill materialism in people's minds thoroughly. I think this is a positive side to them.

Also, there is a sense of security associated with the royal or imperial families; even if a revolution occurs and the government is overthrown, the fundamental character of the nation can remain intact.

This is Japanese wisdom, you see. The idea is that even if the shogunate changed one after another, the existence of the imperial family ensured the stability of Japan's national structure.

I think you must do your best to ensure that the imperial family does not become a vassal to China and does not make an act of homage to China.

Will religions join their forces from now on?

METATRON

I think it may not be easy for Happy Science to find the best way. You have formed a political party and expressed opinions, which considerably influenced the basic ideas of the government. Yet, some forces don't want you to participate in the government, including the LDP, which is somewhat jealous of you, and they don't want to lose their own votes.

Komeito, well, historically speaking, is a party that has already disintegrated. Everything they did has backfired and worked negatively. I think this party is impeding policies regarding China. Hmm... I think they (the government) can't take an anti-China stance because Komeito is the bottleneck.

As for us, hopefully, it will become clear that what the party has been doing is fundamentally wrong. And we are hoping the Happiness Realization Party will at least take over Komeito's seats.

Well, when it collapses, it will happen very quickly. Because if the party has been pro-China for a long time and the results turn out to be disappointing, then...

The party itself is also in turmoil right now. It is quite shaky inside, and even the followers of Soka Gakkai (SGI), the party's foundation, feel envious of Happy Science. For them, you appear to be quite advanced and shining brightly. Moreover, other religions can't say anything about current affairs, so I think they are envious of Happy Science, which can say something about what's happening in the world.

I believe there is a possibility that such religious forces will reunite and become powerful.

C

You just mentioned "uniting the religious forces," but how would you foresee the future in this regard?

METATRON

Well, I think it would be good to envision absorbing all the Buddhist and Shintoist forces.

C

Oh, you mean absorbing the Buddhist and Shinto groups?

METATRON

Yes. At least all of them. Christians can probably be incorporated, too.

C

Really? Christians, too?

METATRON

Japanese Christians can be incorporated, yes. Christianity in Japan has become so "Japanized" compared to the original Christianity. They are happy enough if people celebrate Christmas.

Well, I think that you can probably incorporate Japanese Buddhists, Christians, and Shintoists.

I would suggest a strategy to incorporate these three by the end of this century fully. This is the basic. Then, it will be possible to form politics or political parties based on religion. So, Happy Science should consider taking them in.

Many Shintoist priests read books of Happy Science. There are also many readers among Buddhist temple masters. Christians, too.

If these religious people come to the point where they acknowledge the Savior or the birth of God, then I think their forces will change into political power.

At the moment, I suppose that they are supporting the Liberal Democratic Party and various other parties, though.

C

Would that mean that under the fact, "Lord El Cantare descended on earth as the Supreme Being," the religious and ideological diversity and differences will be integrated at the fundamental level? Would it be a correct understanding?

METATRON

Yes. Let me take an example of a Japanese actress who is said to be a believer of Soka Gakkai. Her guardian spirit has come to Happy Science and is making suggestions.

She said, "I was born a follower of Soka Gakkai because my parents are its staff members, but I love Shakyamuni Buddha. Soka Gakkai says that Nichiren is more important than Shakyamuni, but I don't think so. I believe that Buddhism came into existence because of Shakyamuni Buddha and that the Nichiren sect is only a part of Buddhism. If you can preach the teachings of Buddha, many Soka Gakkai members will become favorable toward Happy Science."

I think this would describe how their younger members feel. Well, among these new religions, I think many of them can be incorporated.

The time has come to put an end to the allergy to religion

METATRON

I think you have to work harder and increase your abilities to transmit your opinions. You also need to strengthen the practical skills of the disciples to build up the organization.

Although there was a kind of allergy to religion in the post-war era, I think you have to overcome this allergy and the prejudice that says religion is evil. In particular, people had the idea that new religions were evil. Well, it is true that a lot of weird religions exist and that there is a need to weed them out. But there is also the need to understand the differences between religions.

Although ambiguously, people have some understanding. Even the newspapers and TV stations are somewhat aware of the differences among religions. They know about the difference between Happy Science and other religions to some extent. They are aware of the difference.

In Japan, religion is supposed to be something that is covered by the weekly magazines and sports papers but not by the major newspapers and TV stations. On the other hand, many religion-based political parties are active in other countries.

From the perspective of India, for example, Japan must look very strange, like a kind of wonderland. When a religious group like Happy Science has been established and is active, trying to ignore it and prevent its advancement into the political field would be beyond their comprehension. They would say, "We can't understand why they have to be held in check. If something new and better comes out, why don't we just go with it?"

I think you will have to make people with such thinking your friends.

Indeed, there is a lot of work to be done. It is one option to gain international understanding and support, but an opinion leader is the best person to boldly bring forth Japan's policy.

I think it's a good thing that Master Ryuho Okawa is getting older and seasoned. At the moment, the prime minister is still a few years older than him, but soon he will be about the same age as prime ministers or older. At that time, I think the number of people who will listen to him will increase considerably.

In business corporations, people in their 60s are usually at the top, so the time will come soon for Master Okawa to gain authority truly. At that time, it is crucial for you to have the power to involve various forces under your umbrella readily.

I think it is the disciples' responsibility to make efforts to enhance the capacity of the organization to incorporate various people.

We will do what we can to help, but that will be with many rough tricks and big tricks when we do. Therefore, we are not entirely sure if our help will be genuinely beneficial for you. Well, unless you do what you can with your human efforts, making changes to details often influences the whole, so you won't know whether our help will be positive or negative.

7
A Message from the "Gods of Genesis"

Why must we make the world on earth the place where the good side wins?

A

I'm afraid we're running out of time, but I wonder if you could share with us any guiding principles or a message for the people of Japan and the world in the 21st century as we enter the space age?

There are many political issues right now, but I believe spiritual values are extremely important. I think the problems of coronavirus are occurring as a challenge for the human race. I would appreciate it if you could share your thoughts.

METATRON

There are taboos regarding military matters, so it's not easy to say clearly, but let us look at the world from a spiritual point of view. With the worldview that there is God or Buddha and high-level spirits in the spiritual world and that human souls undergo reincarnation, the decision of whether to make this world on earth a "good world" or an "evil world" is an important one.

If an evil world is brought about, reincarnation will produce many bad people, and the forces of hell will increase. Well, this is a simple scheme.

Only religion can propagate the idea of choosing good and abandoning evil to make this world on earth a place where good wins over evil. You have to do this.

Even with the laws, the judges can't tell good from evil. This happens because the law is decided in light of the majority of people's opinions, so it is necessary to trace back to the sources of the law. I think you need to keep spreading spiritual values.

In that sense, if the spiritual world and spiritual values are not acknowledged, it will be impossible to tell whether China is good or evil.

They would say, "After the restoration of diplomatic relations between China and Japan, our economy showed rapid recovery and development, and science has advanced, as well. What's wrong with that? The population has increased, wealth has increased, and there are more and more affluent people. Many people in China are much richer than the Japanese."

That is not really communism, but the Chinese call it "communism" because their national character is not being ashamed of telling lies. In fact, the Communist Party members are the "aristocracy," aren't they? The national structure of China is controlled by the aristocratic Communist Party members, with its head as the "Emperor." This system can be expressed as a "mutated communism," don't you think?

It would be best if you made sure that people understand the true nature of that country. I think it is necessary to clarify the truth about the evil that Mao Zedong did and the evil that Xi Jinping is doing. The media can be repulsive, but they have significance in maintaining transparency.

Taking the example of what happened in Tiananmen Square, whether it is just over 300 people, 3,000 people, or 10,000 who died, their family members have a duty and a right to know the truth.

Even if 10,000 people had died, if the authorities said, "There were 300 victims," then the people had no choice but to swallow what they were told. False history has been written, and people have to memorize it. It's also included in university entrance exams. In this way, people are brainwashed, and there is no end to it.

Create a "free market of thoughts" in China

METATRON

Chinese history written in Japan is translated in Taiwan, and then the Taiwanese translation is translated again in mainland China. When Chinese people read it, they will say, "Huh? I didn't know Chinese history was like this. It's totally different from what I was taught."

The current government has rewritten the entire history to suit their needs, and that's the only history their people know. Even in such a big country, there is only one version of the textbook. People are brainwashed with the same textbook.

Their country had been torn apart, and it had been their long-held desire to unify it. The starting point was Shi Huangdi (the first emperor of the Qin Dynasty). But the first emperor, who created a unified state and identified himself as "emperor," reigned for only 12 years. His son's reign merely lasted for three years, so the Qin Dynasty had only 15 years of history.

Even if the country's unification is valued, the regime only causes many people's misery, so the ruler is constantly under the threat of assassination. It is crucial to reveal the actual situation of the regime, where the leader is under the threat of assassination domestically while being subject to foreign assaults. At the same time, it is necessary to create a "free market of thoughts" through the exchange of cultural products such as movies, novels, or anything else, so that all kinds of things can come in without being impeded by barriers.

Now, if anything, they are even working behind the scenes to get Hollywood to support Chinese values by getting Chinese actors to perform in Hollywood movies.

If China gives its blessings, Hollywood movies will have an audience of 900 million people in China because 900 million out of 1.4 billion can afford to watch movies. It's such a big market. So, they have been encroaching on the world market from the cultural front.

I don't think the Japanese would dare to do this kind of thing. If Mr. Suga were a real Machiavellist, he would have to work out such a strategy, but he hasn't gone that far yet.

The time when we need to create something new has come

METATRON

Having said that, what you will have to bear in mind now is...

First, you will have to clarify "what God or Buddha considers to be good and evil," "what constitutes wisdom," and "what constitutes virtue." You will also have to clarify the structure of the world, the system of reincarnation, the structure of the spiritual world and this world, and the structure of the world in relation to the universe. In this way, I believe you will be able to bring about a kind of innovative change in people's consciousness. You need to bring about this movement on a global scale.

I would like to see this happening, especially in major countries. You need to make this happen in the influential countries that can propagate information.

Then it leads to a conclusion that your international headquarters is still not powerful enough, nor does it have enough budget.

I think you need to think about how to incorporate other religions in this movement by the end of this century. You will also need to expand more and more internationally, so you need to modernize the way you operate.

The time has come when you need to discard almost all thoughts created in the 20th century and instead create something new.

A

A lot is expected of Happy Science's mission, right?

How can we subdue the pride of the earthlings who have become so conceited?

C

With the advancement of materialism and science and technology, the power of belief seems to weaken among all human races. From the guidance we received from you in the previous eight or nine sessions, Mr. Metatron, I've understood that the keyword is "to believe."

I would appreciate it if you could tell us about the mindset we must ensure. That is, I would like to know about religious points that enable human beings to leap forward or make a breakthrough toward "believing."

METATRON

Oh, you know, I don't want to reveal too much of our strategies. But we are, in fact, the equivalent to the "gods of Genesis" in your world.

We are the gods of Genesis, meaning that we are the ones who have been creating. Like the gods of the Book of Genesis, we have created civilizations on various planets, humanity's history, and people's history in outer space.

The problem with the people of the Earth right now is that they have become so arrogant.

C

Everyone is like *tengu*, the long-nosed goblins?

METATRON

Yes. People have become conceited like *tengu*. They are proud of having received education to become technical experts. People of the Earth seem to think they can control everything, from the bottom of the ocean to the sky. They seem to believe they can develop anything with the almighty power of science. In short, they have become *tengu*. The whole population has already become long-nosed goblins, so we must do something to crush this.

There are several ways when considering what we can do to flatten the *tengu*'s nose or subdue the pride of those who have become so proud of themselves. Well, there are ways, but if I show our hand too much, you might be a little shocked. So, well, I can't tell you, but you must know that when a Messiah arrives, it is also a time of crisis.

C

A time of crisis?

METATRON

Yes. Several crises will be brought about.

The coronavirus pandemic is one of them, but this is not the end. Another will follow the next crisis, and other ones throughout the 21st century, there will be a lot of them. Each time, the crisis will create a situation that will make people think that humanity alone may not be able to cope with it anymore.

I won't go into the details of the whole picture, but the voice of God will be heard. "What He is thinking" will be heard.

The point is, "if you follow it, you can get out of that crisis, but if you don't listen, something catastrophic may happen."

Well, we intend to subject human beings to a "test" to make a choice.

There is a move to appreciate Chinese values and spread them to Asia, Europe, Japan, and even the United States to bring those countries down. We have already presented a standard for judging good and evil.

We are watching over you to see which choice you will make, but there will surely be many more disasters if you make the wrong one.

It's time to correct the false notion of separation of church and state

B

In that case, spreading the Truth to the major countries, not to mention across Japan, will be very important, right?

METATRON

That's right.

The current level of your missionary work is far from satisfactory. Ideally, you need to have the power that is equivalent to the government.

Think about the era when the Great Buddha of Nara was erected. Faith was the matter of the national project, and in order to save the people, faith was essential. Faith was toward Buddha, and it was represented through the building of the Great Buddha. The project was a symbol of national unity, the unity of people.

I'm not wholly against the imperial family, as its existence is undoubtedly valuable. However, since the new teachings of El Cantare are being preached now, it is vital to create something that symbolizes this and make His teachings clear to the people. Also, you need to spread the teachings worldwide, breaking through existing frameworks and regulations.

But, well, I think some of such moves are already starting to happen.

Take the example of HSU (Happy Science University). It functions well as a university, even if the state, or Ministry of Education, Culture, Sports, Science, and Technology, does not approve it. Its graduates have found jobs and are currently working. If more and more people believe in the university, it will not be a matter of whether the state approves it or not. Effectively...

The truth is, the private sector or rather private universities can be established freely. If it's a state-run university or one subsidized by taxpayers' money, it has to operate according to what the state decides. But private universities are free to decide what they want to produce. They are as free as business corporations, so the authorities don't have the right to control them, nor do they have the right to order them around.

The authorities want to uniformly regulate universities to secure places where retired public officers can find employment under the pretext of providing subsidies. You are trying to break down this system. In fact, there is no way they can find a position in HSU, Happy Science University. The officials cannot seek employment because they don't belong to your belief system.

Since they cannot currently find post-retirement employment in HSU, they are trying to turn the university into an ordinary school where anyone can enter. They are trying to use subsidies as bait to get what they want, but you resist, right? Well, I think you must adhere to your principle.

Your political party (the Happiness Realization Party) may keep on losing (in the national elections), but it continues to express its opinions without compromising its principles. *The Liberty* magazine is on its side. As you maintain your attitude, more and more people will come to recognize its presence.

A political party doesn't only mean the one that receives political subsidies. A political party must have a specific opinion, and it is a place where people come together to engage in political activities, right?

Some people are allergic to what you are saying because the idea of "separation of church and state" is now firmly incorporated in the Japanese Constitution. But you have to refute and say, "This is a wrong notion in the first place. Let's clarify the history of Japan. There has never been a time when separation of church and state was practiced. This system was implemented only after the war."

General Douglas MacArthur himself, who initiated the policy attempted to change it, as he himself thought the system should not remain in place. It follows that the pre-war Japanese system wasn't entirely wrong.

The majority of Americans believe Japan became a democratic nation as a result of losing the war after the atomic bombs were dropped. More than 90% of Americans believe this. But in reality, there was already "Taisho Democracy[3]." Even in the Meiji era (1868-1912), people were talking about the equality of all people.

Japan had been trying to change and become a democracy. In fact, it had already been accepted as one of the five major powers in the world. Japan was one of the five major powers, which might be the equivalent of the present-day G7 countries. It was entrusted with the management of China and the Korean Peninsula by the West.

The influence of evil aliens behind the Second World War

METATRON

Finally, the war with the United States was not a "war of aggression" but a "war of hegemony" in any way. Because when the war started, Japan's military power was superior to that of the United States. Japan's naval power was far superior, too. It was definitely a war for supremacy. Americans converted their industrial power, which they used to manufacture automobiles for military purposes.

They were the ones who triggered the Great Depression of 1929. In a way, the situation back then is similar to the current situation because there is a culprit that developed the coronavirus. The United States was the one that caused the global recession at that time. To overcome the global recession they caused, Americans transformed themselves into a military nation and boosted the military industry.

The general claim that "building dams in the Tennessee Valley helped the economy recover" was not valid, as the project had no effect at all. The truth is, they created military industries on a large scale and transformed the automobile industry into the military industry. They dropped a lot of bombs and made a lot of airplanes and warships. Because war is a great "consumption industry," they could consume more and more and produce new things. It was how their 10-year-long recession finally ended.

The Great Recession in the United States began in 1929 and ended as Germany started invasion in 1939, and finally, Japan participated in the war in 1941.

It could be said Germany and Japan were the "savior" for the United States because they participated in the war, and consequently, the recession ended. In this respect, it has gradually become clear that Franklin Roosevelt's strategy dragged them into the war.

Moreover, we now know that the evil aliens in China we are currently fighting were also inside the United States.

B

Thank you. It's clear now. When you say, "they were inside the United States," does that mean the evil aliens influenced President Roosevelt?

METATRON

Yes, he was influenced.

B

Oh, really, he was affected?

METATRON

That's right.

A

Thank you for the clarification.

METATRON

So, although the history created by the U.S. side is now supposed to be entirely correct, this is not true.

Roosevelt should have been appointed president with the promise that there would be no involvement in foreign wars if he were re-elected. But in reality, he was the one who plotted to start the war. Similar to what China is doing now, he was the mastermind behind the strategy to drag Japan and Germany as well as the Soviet Union into the war. I think you have to reveal the truth about this.

B

It's so intricate and...

METATRON

"Xi Jinping X" in its previous form definitely affected Roosevelt.

B

I see.

METATRON

Yes, and that was not a spiritual possession but a walk-in.

C

"Xi Jinping X" walked in?

METATRON

Yes. Roosevelt was transformed halfway through. In the face of the Great Recession, he had run out of options and could no longer pretend that he cared about justice. In this way, he was transformed to save the Americans. As a result, Japan had to sacrifice three million of its people.

C

So, that's where the truth of history lies.

What is expected of Japan now?

METATRON

I think there were also some mistakes you should reflect on.

What Japan is expected of now is, well, what you call "defense capability." As such, Japan needs at least enough defense capability to protect its fellow Asians who are not tainted by false notions.

Also, I think Japan must create a framework that enables it to cooperate with the Western countries when they take action on what they believe is right.

Moreover, I would like the provision that stipulates the separation of church and state to be reformed if possible.

Religions should be founded on the belief that people are inherently good. Well, some wrong religions are almost like frauds, but they will automatically be eliminated as good religions grow.

You must make a point and say, "Just as the bad opinions fade away when different opinions contend with one another, the good religions should expel bad religions like white blood cells eating away foreign substances. It is a mistake to think that the state should regulate them."

Along with Article 9, I believe that the provision that stipulates separation of church and state should be eliminated from the Constitution. Initially, it must have been implemented to keep a check on state sponsorship of Shintoism.

People may think it is wrong for religions to engage in politics, but it is not. Soka Gakkai, which is not even a religion, is only acting like a religion. They have no doctrine or a religious leader.

The person at the top of their organization is what you would call the director of activity promotion. Historically, what they call a chairman has been the leader of activity promotion. They propagate their claims, but if asked, "What is the purpose of spreading our ideas?" no one would be able to provide a convincing answer. This is how Soka Gakkai is. They only have the finance division and the activity promotion division.

Besides, the books they publish are written by different people. Their editorial division doesn't transcribe and publish the president's words. Their job is to "fabricate the president's words as if they were told."

Right now, I'm here to talk with you, but even without this fact, the other religion is working on writing books as if the leader spoke about something.

I think it's essential to clearly distinguish between black and white regarding these disreputable fake religions.

A

Yes, indeed. Thank you very much for your valuable guidance today.

RYUHO OKAWA

Thank you very much [*claps twice*].

Afterword

The Tokyo Olympic Games have started. The occasion coincided with the upsurge of the fifth wave of the coronavirus pandemic.

The outcome is as I anticipated, yet it is tragic.

The currently used coronavirus vaccines will not have the power to prevent the fifth wave, much less the sixth and seventh waves. If I use an analogy, the current situation is as if the Japan Self-Defense Forces respond to the enemy firing missiles from the Pacific Ocean by firing PAC-3 missiles into the opposite Sea of Japan side instead, simply because the system is deployed there. New variants of the coronavirus keep emerging, but all we have are irrelevant measures.

Unless global justice is established, there will be no end to the coronavirus crisis, earthquakes, heavy rains, floods, and heatwaves. This situation is not due to "CO2" but because the life consciousness of planet Earth itself wants to reduce the number of about eight billion humans infesting its surface.

Increase the good and decrease the evil. Strengthen faith in God or Buddha. Stop the proliferation of those who have become conceited due to the progress of materialistic science. The light of the future will never shine on those who scoff at the words of the Savior.

Ryuho Okawa
Master & CEO of Happy Science Group
July 23, 2021

TRANSLATOR'S NOTES

1 Prime Minister Suga resigned on October 4, 2021.

2 The Japanese general election was held on October 31.

3 Taisho democracy:

The term for a liberal and democratic movement across political, economic, and cultural areas in Japan during the Taisho period (1912-1926). The tax qualification for voting was reduced, which allowed more people to vote, and eventually eliminated in 1925. Political parties were formed and legislation favorable to labor was passed.

ABOUT THE AUTHOR

RYUHO OKAWA was born on July 7th 1956, in Tokushima, Japan. After graduating from the University of Tokyo with a law degree, he joined a Tokyo-based trading house. While working at its New York headquarters, he studied international finance at the Graduate Center of the City University of New York. In 1981, he attained Great Enlightenment and became aware that he is El Cantare with a mission to bring salvation to all humankind. In 1986, he established Happy Science. It now has members in over 160 countries across the world, with more than 700 branches and temples as well as 10,000 missionary houses around the world. The total number of lectures has exceeded 3,350 (of which more than 150 are in English) and over 2,900 books (of which more than 600 are Spiritual Interview Series) have been published, many of which are translated into 37 languages. Many of the books, including *The Laws of the Sun* have become best sellers or million sellers. To date, Happy Science has produced 24 movies. The original story and original concept were given by the Executive Producer Ryuho Okawa. Recent movie titles are *Into the Dreams...and Horror Experiences* (live-action, August 2021), *The Laws of the Universe - The Age of Elohim* (animation movie, October 2021), *Aikokujoshi—Kurenai Bushido* (literally, "Patriot Girl—The True Bushido Spirit," live-action movie scheduled to be released in February 2022). He has also composed the lyrics and music of over 450 songs, such as theme songs and featured songs of movies. Moreover, he is the Founder of Happy Science University and Happy Science Academy (Junior and Senior High School), Founder and President of the Happiness Realization Party, Founder and Honorary Headmaster of Happy Science Institute of Government and Management, Founder of IRH Press Co., Ltd., and the Chairperson of NEW STAR PRODUCTION Co., Ltd. and ARI Production Co., Ltd.

WHAT IS EL CANTARE?

El Cantare means "the Light of the Earth," and is the Supreme God of the Earth who has been guiding humankind since the beginning of Genesis. He is whom Jesus called Father and Muhammad called Allah, and is the Creator in Shintoism, *Ame-no-Mioya-Gami*. Different parts of El Cantare's core consciousness have descended to Earth in the past, once as Alpha and another as Elohim. His branch spirits, such as Shakyamuni Buddha and Hermes, have descended to Earth many times and helped to flourish many civilizations. To unite various religions and to integrate various fields of study in order to build a new civilization on Earth, a part of the core consciousness has descended to Earth as Master Ryuho Okawa.

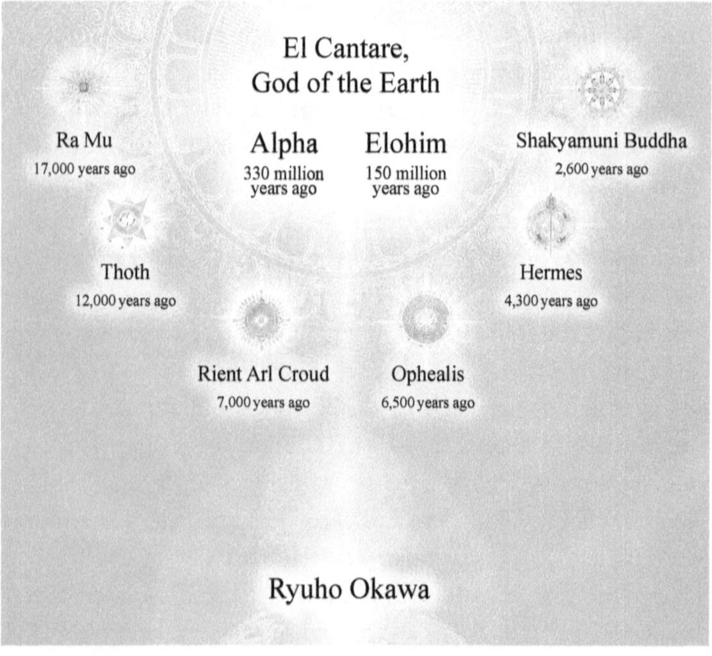

Alpha is a part of the core consciousness of El Cantare who descended to Earth around 330 million years ago. Alpha preached Earth's Truths to harmonize and unify Earth-born humans and space people who came from other planets.

Elohim is a part of El Cantare's core consciousness who descended to Earth around 150 million years ago. He gave wisdom, mainly on the differences of light and darkness, good and evil.

Shakyamuni Buddha was born as a prince into the Shakya Clan in India around 2,600 years ago. When he was 29 years old, he renounced the world and sought enlightenment. He later attained Great Enlightenment and founded Buddhism.

Hermes is one of the 12 Olympian gods in Greek mythology, but the spiritual Truth is that he taught the teachings of love and progress around 4,300 years ago that became the origin of the current Western civilization. He is a hero that truly existed.

Ophealis was born in Greece around 6,500 years ago and was the leader who took an expedition to as far as Egypt. He is the God of miracles, prosperity, and arts, and is known as Osiris in the Egyptian mythology.

Rient Arl Croud was born as a king of the ancient Incan Empire around 7,000 years ago and taught about the mysteries of the mind. In the heavenly world, he is responsible for the interactions that take place between various planets.

Thoth was an almighty leader who built the golden age of the Atlantic civilization around 12,000 years ago. In the Egyptian mythology, he is known as god Thoth.

Ra Mu was a leader who built the golden age of the civilization of Mu around 17,000 years ago. As a religious leader and a politician, he ruled by uniting religion and politics.

WHAT IS A SPIRITUAL MESSAGE?

We are all spiritual beings living on this earth. The following is the mechanism behind Master Ryuho Okawa's spiritual messages.

1 You are a spirit

People are born into this world to gain wisdom through various experiences and return to the other world when their lives end. We are all spirits and repeat this cycle in order to refine our souls.

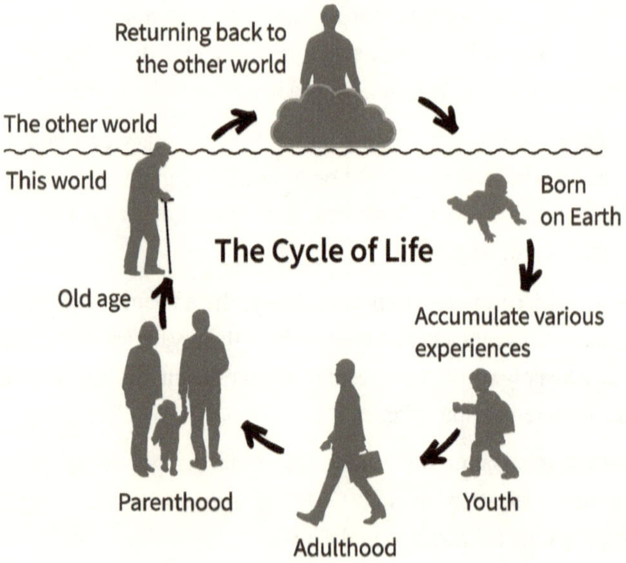

2 You have a guardian spirit

Guardian spirits are those who protect the people who are living on this earth. Each of us has a guardian spirit that watches over us and guides us from the other world. They were us in our past life, and are identical in how we think.

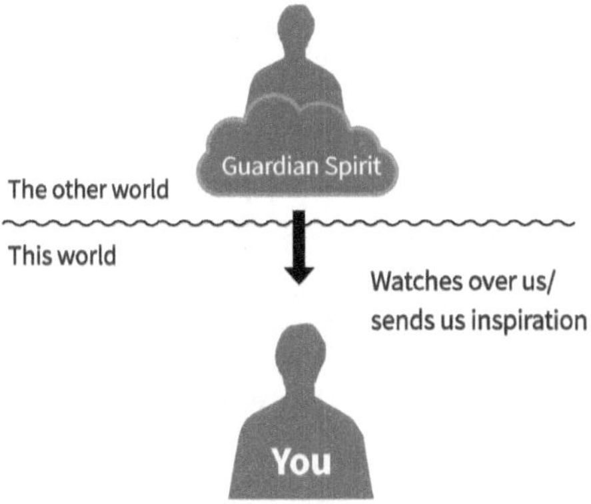

3 How spiritual messages work

Master Ryuho Okawa, through his enlightenment, is capable of summoning any spirit from anywhere in the world, including the spirit world.

Master Okawa's way of receiving spiritual messages is fundamentally different from that of other psychic mediums who undergo trances and are thereby completely taken over by the spirits they are channeling.

Master Okawa's attainment of a high level of enlightenment enables him to retain full control of his consciousness and body throughout the duration of the spiritual message. To allow the spirits to express their own thoughts and personalities freely, however, Master Okawa usually softens the dominancy of his consciousness. This way, he is able to keep his own philosophies out of the way and ensure that the spiritual messages are pure expressions of the spirits he is channeling.

Since guardian spirits think at the same subconscious level as the person living on earth, Master Okawa can summon the spirit and find out what the person on earth is actually thinking. If the person has already returned to the other world, the spirit can give messages to the people living on earth through Master Okawa.

Since 2009, more than 1,200 sessions of spiritual messages have been openly recorded by Master Okawa, and the majority of these have been published. Spiritual messages from the guardian spirits of people living today such as Donald Trump, former Japanese Prime Minister Shinzo Abe and Chinese President Xi Jinping, as well as spiritual messages sent from the spirit world by Jesus Christ, Muhammad, Thomas Edison, Mother Teresa, Steve Jobs and Nelson Mandela are just a tiny pack of spiritual messages that were published so far.

Domestically, in Japan, these spiritual messages are being read by a wide range of politicians and mass media, and the high-level contents of these books are delivering an impact even more on politics, news and public opinion. In recent years, there have been spiritual messages recorded in English, and English translations are being done on the spiritual messages given in Japanese. These have been published overseas, one after another, and have started to shake the world.

...
...
❶ The guardian spirit / spirit in the other world...
❷ Goes inside Master Okawa in this world
❸ Master Okawa speaks the words of the guardian spirit / spirit

For more about spiritual messages and a complete list of books in the Spiritual Interview Series, visit *okawabooks.com*

ABOUT HAPPY SCIENCE

Happy Science is a global movement that empowers individuals to find purpose and spiritual happiness and to share that happiness with their families, societies, and the world. With more than 12 million members around the world, Happy Science aims to increase awareness of spiritual truths and expand our capacity for love, compassion, and joy so that together we can create the kind of world we all wish to live in.

Activities at Happy Science are based on the Principle of Happiness (Love, Wisdom, Self-Reflection, and Progress). This principle embraces worldwide philosophies and beliefs, transcending boundaries of culture and religions.

Love teaches us to give ourselves freely without expecting anything in return; it encompasses giving, nurturing, and forgiving.

Wisdom leads us to the insights of spiritual truths, and opens us to the true meaning of life and the will of God (the universe, the highest power, Buddha).

Self-Reflection brings a mindful, nonjudgmental lens to our thoughts and actions to help us find our truest selves—the essence of our souls—and deepen our connection to the highest power. It helps us attain a clean and peaceful mind and leads us to the right life path.

Progress emphasizes the positive, dynamic aspects of our spiritual growth—actions we can take to manifest and spread happiness around the world. It's a path that not only expands our soul growth, but also furthers the collective potential of the world we live in.

PROGRAMS AND EVENTS

The doors of Happy Science are open to all. We offer a variety of programs and events, including self-exploration and self-growth programs, spiritual seminars, meditation and contemplation sessions, study groups, and book events.

Our programs are designed to:

* Deepen your understanding of your purpose and meaning in life
* Improve your relationships and increase your capacity to love unconditionally
* Attain peace of mind, decrease anxiety and stress, and feel positive
* Gain deeper insights and a broader perspective on the world
* Learn how to overcome life's challenges

... and much more.

For more information, visit happy-science.org.

ABOUT HAPPINESS REALIZATION PARTY

The Happiness Realization Party (HRP) was founded in May 2009 by Master Ryuho Okawa as part of the Happy Science Group. HRP strives to improve the Japanese society, based on three basic political principles of "freedom, democracy, and faith," and let Japan promote individual and public happiness from Asia to the world as a leader nation.

1) Diplomacy and Security: Protecting Freedom, Democracy, and Faith of Japan and the World from China's Totalitarianism

Japan's current defense system is insufficient against China's expanding hegemony and the threat of North Korea's nuclear missiles. Japan, as the leader of Asia, must strengthen its defense power and promote strategic diplomacy together with the nations which share the values of freedom, democracy, and faith. Further, HRP aims to realize world peace under the leadership of Japan, the nation with the spirit of religious tolerance.

2) Economy: Early economic recovery through utilizing the "wisdom of the private sector"

Economy has been damaged severely by the novel coronavirus originated in China. Many companies have been forced into bankruptcy or out of business. What is needed for economic recovery now is not subsidies and regulations by the government, but policies which can utilize the "wisdom of the private sector."

For more information, visit en.hr-party.jp

HAPPY SCIENCE ACADEMY JUNIOR AND SENIOR HIGH SCHOOL

Happy Science Academy Junior and Senior High School is a boarding school founded with the goal of educating the future leaders of the world who can have a big vision, persevere, and take on new challenges.

Currently, there are two campuses in Japan; the Nasu Main Campus in Tochigi Prefecture, founded in 2010, and the Kansai Campus in Shiga Prefecture, founded in 2013.

CONTACT INFORMATION

Happy Science is a worldwide organization with faith centers around the globe. For a comprehensive list of centers, visit the worldwide directory at *happy-science.org*. The following are some of the many Happy Science locations:

United States and Canada

New York
79 Franklin St., New York, NY 10013
Phone: 212-343-7972
Fax: 212-343-7973
Email: ny@happy-science.org
Website: happyscience-usa.org

New Jersey
725 River Rd, #102B, Edgewater, NJ 07020
Phone: 201-313-0127
Fax: 201-313-0120
Email: nj@happy-science.org
Website: happyscience-usa.org

Florida
5208 8th St., Zephyrhills, FL 33542
Phone: 813-715-0000
Fax: 813-715-0010
Email: florida@happy-science.org
Website: happyscience-usa.org

Atlanta
1874 Piedmont Ave., NE Suite 360-C
Atlanta, GA 30324
Phone: 404-892-7770
Email: atlanta@happy-science.org
Website: happyscience-usa.org

San Francisco
525 Clinton St.
Redwood City, CA 94062
Phone & Fax: 650-363-2777
Email: sf@happy-science.org
Website: happyscience-usa.org

Los Angeles
1590 E. Del Mar Blvd., Pasadena, CA 91106
Phone: 626-395-7775
Fax: 626-395-7776
Email: la@happy-science.org
Website: happyscience-usa.org

Orange County
10231 Slater Ave., #204
Fountain Valley, CA 92708
Phone: 714-659-1501
Email: oc@happy-science.org
Website: happyscience-usa.org

San Diego
7841 Balboa Ave., Suite #202
San Diego, CA 92111
Phone: 626-395-7775
Fax: 626-395-7776
E-mail: sandiego@happy-science.org
Website: happyscience-usa.org

Hawaii
Phone: 808-591-9772
Fax: 808-591-9776
Email: hi@happy-science.org
Website: happyscience-usa.org

Kauai
3343 Kanakolu Street, Suite 5
Lihue, HI 96766, U.S.A.
Phone: 808-822-7007
Fax: 808-822-6007
Email: kauai-hi@happy-science.org
Website: happyscience-usa.org

Toronto
845 The Queensway
Etobicoke ON M8Z 1N6 Canada
Phone: 1-416-901-3747
Email: toronto@happy-science.org
Website: happy-science.ca

Vancouver
#201-2607 East 49th Avenue
Vancouver, BC, V5S 1J9, Canada
Phone: 1-604-437-7735
Fax: 1-604-437-7764
Email: vancouver@happy-science.org
Website: happy-science.ca

International

Tokyo
1-6-7 Togoshi, Shinagawa
Tokyo, 142-0041 Japan
Phone: 81-3-6384-5770
Fax: 81-3-6384-5776
Email: tokyo@happy-science.org
Website: happy-science.org

Seoul
74, Sadang-ro 27-gil,
Dongjak-gu, Seoul, Korea
Phone: 82-2-3478-8777
Fax: 82-2-3478-9777
Email: korea@happy-science.org
Website: happyscience-korea.org

London
3 Margaret St.
London,W1W 8RE United Kingdom
Phone: 44-20-7323-9255
Fax: 44-20-7323-9344
Email: eu@happy-science.org
Website: happyscience-uk.org

Taipei
No. 89, Lane 155, Dunhua N. Road
Songshan District, Taipei City 105, Taiwan
Phone: 886-2-2719-9377
Fax: 886-2-2719-5570
Email: taiwan@happy-science.org
Website: happyscience-tw.org

Sydney
516 Pacific Hwy, Lane Cove North,
NSW 2066, Australia
Phone: 61-2-9411-2877
Fax: 61-2-9411-2822
Email: sydney@happy-science.org

Malaysia
No 22A, Block 2, Jalil Link Jalan Jalil
Jaya 2, Bukit Jalil 57000, Kuala Lumpur, Malaysia
Phone: 60-3-8998-7877
Fax: 60-3-8998-7977
Email: malaysia@happy-science.org
Website: happyscience.org.my

Brazil Headquarters
Rua. Domingos de Morais 1154,
Vila Mariana, Sao Paulo SP
CEP 04010-100, Brazil
Phone: 55-11-5088-3800
Email: sp@happy-science.org
Website: happyscience.com.br

Nepal
Kathmandu Metropolitan City Ward
No. 15,
Ring Road, Kimdol,
Sitapaila Kathmandu, Nepal
Phone: 97-714-272931
Email: nepal@happy-science.org

Jundiai
Rua Congo, 447, Jd. Bonfiglioli
Jundiai-CEP, 13207-340
Phone: 55-11-4587-5952
Email: jundiai@happy-science.org

Uganda
Plot 877 Rubaga Road, Kampala
P.O. Box 34130, Kampala, Uganda
Phone: 256-79-4682-121
Email: uganda@happy-science.org
Website: happyscience-uganda.org

ABOUT IRH PRESS

IRH Press Co., Ltd., based in Tokyo, was founded in 1987 as a publishing division of Happy Science. IRH Press publishes religious and spiritual books, journals, magazines and also operates broadcast and film production enterprises. For more information, visit *okawabooks.com*.

Follow us on:

Facebook: Okawa Books
Twitter: Okawa Books
Goodreads: Ryuho Okawa
Instagram: OkawaBooks
Pinterest: Okawa Books

NEWSLETTER

To receive book related news, promotions and events, please subscribe to our newsletter below.

https://okawabooks.us11.list-manage.com/subscribe?u=1fc70960eefd92668052ab7f8&id=2fbd8150ef

MEDIA

OKAWA BOOK CLUB

A conversation about Ryuho Okawa's titles, topics ranging from self-help, current affairs, spirituality and religions.

Available at iTunes, Spotify and Amazon Music.

Apple iTunes:
https://podcasts.apple.com/us/podcast/okawa-book-club/id1527893043

Spotify:
https://open.spotify.com/show/09mpgX2iJ6stVm4eBRdo2b

Amazon Music:
https://music.amazon.com/podcasts/7b759f24-ff72-4523-bfee-24f48294998f/Okawa-Book-Club

BOOKS BY RYUHO OKAWA

RYUHO OKAWA'S LAWS SERIES

The Laws Series is an annual volume of books that are mainly comprised of Ryuho Okawa's lectures that function as universal guidance to all people. They are of various topics that were given in accordance with the changes that each year brings. *The Laws of the Sun*, the first publication of the laws series, ranked in the annual best-selling list in Japan in 1994. Since, the laws series' titles have ranked in the annual best-selling list every year for more than two decades, setting socio-cultural trends in Japan and around the world.

The 27th Laws Series

THE LAWS OF SECRET

Awaken to This New World and Change Your Life

Paperback • 248 pages • $16.95
ISBN: 978-1-942125-81-5

Our physical world coexists with the multi-dimensional spirit world and we are constantly interacting with some kind of spiritual energy, whether positive or negative, without consciously realizing it. This book reveals how our lives are affected by invisible influences, including the spiritual reasons behind influenza, the novel coronavirus infection, and other illnesses.

The new view of the world in this book will inspire you to change your life in a better direction, and to become someone who can give hope and courage to others in this age of confusion.

For a complete list of books, visit okawabooks.com

THE TRILOGY

The first three volumes of the Laws Series, *The Laws of the Sun*, *The Golden Laws*, and *The Nine Dimensions* make a trilogy that completes the basic framework of the teachings of God's Truths. *The Laws of the Sun* discusses the structure of God's Laws, *The Golden Laws* expounds on the doctrine of time, and *The Nine Dimensions* reveals the nature of space.

THE LAWS OF THE SUN

ONE SOURCE, ONE PLANET, ONE PEOPLE

Paperback • 288 pages • $15.95
ISBN: 978-1-942125-43-3

IMAGINE IF YOU COULD ASK GOD why He created this world and what spiritual laws He used to shape us—and everything around us. If we could understand His designs and intentions, we could discover what our goals in life should be and whether our actions move us closer to those goals or farther away.

At a young age, a spiritual calling prompted Ryuho Okawa to outline what he innately understood to be universal truths for all humankind. In *The Laws of the Sun*, Okawa outlines these laws of the universe and provides a road map for living one's life with greater purpose and meaning.

In this powerful book, Ryuho Okawa reveals the transcendent nature of consciousness and the secrets of our multidimensional universe and our place in it. By understanding the different stages of love and following the Buddhist Eightfold Path, he believes we can speed up our eternal process of development. *The Laws of the Sun* shows the way to realize true happiness—a happiness that continues from this world through the other.

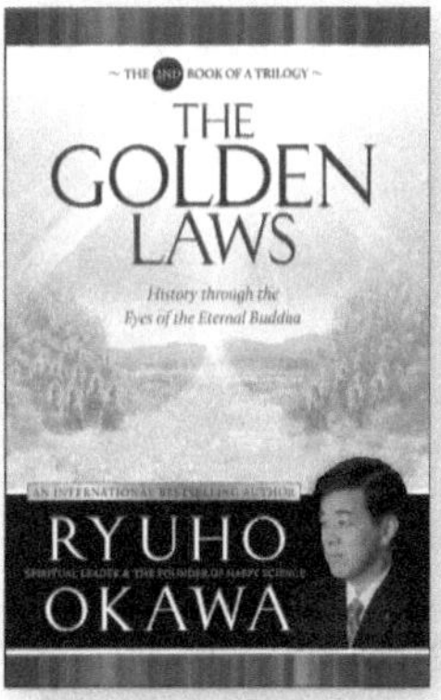

THE GOLDEN LAWS

HISTORY THROUGH THE EYES OF THE ETERNAL BUDDHA

Paperback • 201 pages • $14.95
ISBN: 978-1-941779-81-1

Throughout history, Great Guiding Spirits have been present on Earth in both the East and the West at crucial points in human history to further our spiritual development. *The Golden Laws* reveals how Divine Plan has been unfolding on Earth, and outlines 5,000 years of the secret history of humankind. Once we understand the true course of history, through past, present and into the future, we cannot help but become aware of the significance of our spiritual mission in the present age.

THE NINE DIMENSIONS

UNVEILING THE LAWS OF ETERNITY

Paperback • 168 pages • $15.95
ISBN: 978-0-982698-56-3

This book is a window into the mind of our loving God, who designed this world and the vast, wondrous world of our afterlife as a school with many levels through which our souls learn and grow. When the religions and cultures of the world discover the truth of their common spiritual origin, they will be inspired to accept their differences, come together under faith in God, and build an era of harmony and peaceful progress on Earth.

THE LAWS OF HAPPINESS

LOVE, WISDOM, SELF-REFLECTION AND PROGRESS

Paperback • 264 pages • $16.95
ISBN: 978-1-942125-70-9

What is happiness? In this book, Ryuho Okawa explains that happiness is not found outside us; it's found within us, in how we think, how we look at our lives in this world, what we believe in, and how we devote our hearts to the work we do. Even as we go through suffering and unfavorable circumstances, we can always shift our mindset and become happier by simply giving love instead of taking love.

THE LAWS OF GREAT ENLIGHTENMENT

ALWAYS WALK WITH BUDDHA

Paperback • 232 pages • $17.95
ISBN: 978-1-942125-62-4

Constant self-blame for mistakes, setbacks, or failures and feelings of unforgivingness toward others are hard to overcome. Through the power of enlightenment we can learn to forgive ourselves and others, overcome life's problems, and courageously create a brighter future ourselves. This book addresses the core problems of life that people often struggle with and offers advice on how to overcome them based on spiritual truths.

For a complete list of books, visit okawabooks.com

THE LAWS OF HOPE

THE LIGHT IS HERE

Paperback • 224 pages • $16.95
ISBN:978-1-942125-76-1

This book provides ways to bring light and hope to ourselves through our own efforts, even in the midst of sufferings and adversities. Inspired by a wish to bring happiness, success, and hope to humanity, Okawa shows us how to look at and think about our lives and circumstances. By making efforts in your current circumstances, you can fulfill your mission to shed light on yourself and those around you.

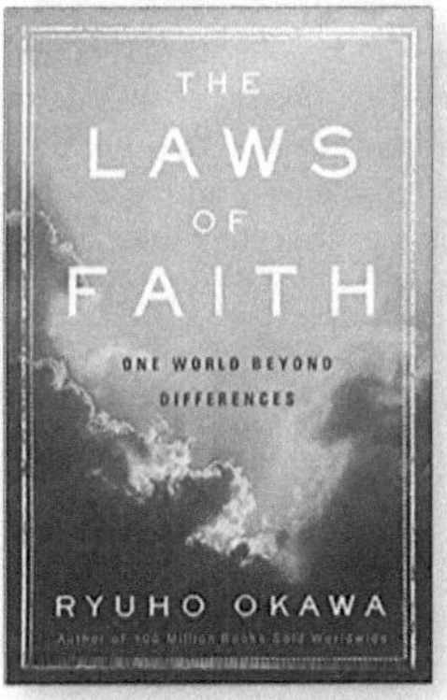

THE LAWS OF FAITH

ONE WORLD BEYOND DIFFERENCES

Paperback • 208 pages • $15.95
ISBN: 978-1-942125-34-1

Ryuho Okawa preaches at the core of a new universal religion from various angles while integrating logical and spiritual viewpoints in mind with current world situations. This book offers us the key to accept diversities beyond differences in ethnicity, religion, race, gender, descent, and so on, harmonize the individuals and nations and create a world filled with peace and prosperity.

RECOMMENDED SPIRITUAL MESSAGES

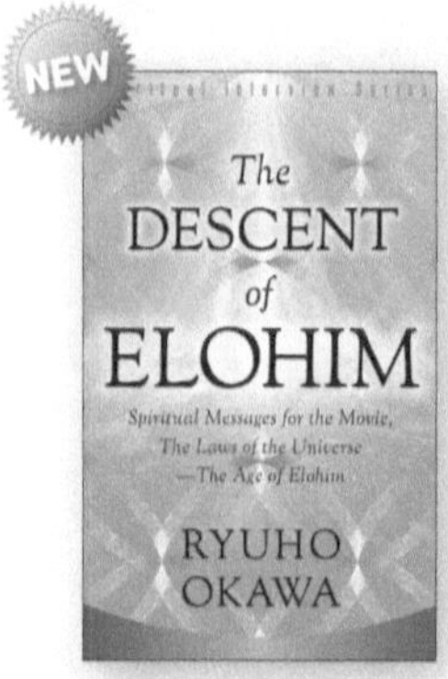

THE DESCENT OF ELOHIM

SPIRITUAL MESSAGES FOR THE MOVIE,
THE LAWS OF THE UNIVERSE-THE AGE OF ELOHIM

Paperback • 160 pages • $11.95
ISBN: 978-1-943928-17-0

This book contains the spiritual messages from Elohim, the Lord who appears in the Old Testament and who actually led His people about 150 million years ago. Through this book and the movie, *The Laws of the Universe - The Age of Elohim*, you can learn how life on Earth was like at that time, and how diverse people, who had come from other planets, fought each other until they finally found peace and harmony under Lord Elohim.

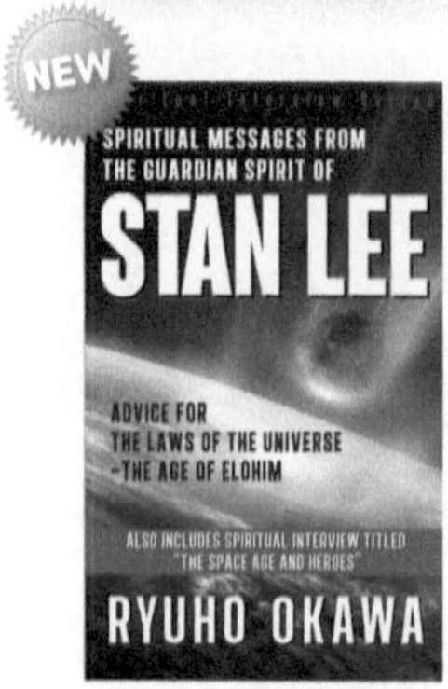

SPIRITUAL MESSAGES FROM THE GUARDIAN SPIRIT OF STAN LEE

ADVICE FOR *THE LAWS OF THE UNIVERSE*
- THE AGE OF ELOHIM

Paperback • 200 pages • $11.95
ISBN: 978-1-943928-16-3

To seek advice on the plot for the movie *The Laws of the Universe - The Age of Elohim*, Okawa summoned the guardian spirit of Stan Lee, the father of Marvel Comics heroes. The guardian spirit of Stan Lee tells how he comes up with the heroes, and gives his insights on the kind of heroes that humans need in the coming Space Age.

SPIRITUAL INTERVIEWS WITH THE GUARDIAN SPIRIT OF GEORGE LUCAS AND THE SPIRIT OF CARRIE FISHER

AWAKENING MESSAGES TO THE SPACE AGE

Paperback • 154 pages • $11.95
ISBN: 978-1943928-14-9

In the world today, a large totalitarian nation is aiming to take control of the world, while small democratic powers are trying to resist its attack. By reading this book, you will realize that similar battles were already happening in outer space, and that the Star Wars Series is a saga based on the real-life stories.

For a complete list of books, visit okawabooks.com

MESSAGES FROM SPACE BEINGS

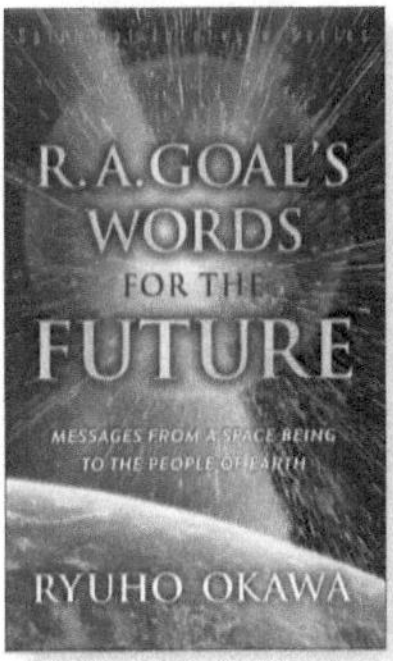

R. A. GOAL'S WORDS FOR THE FUTURE

MESSAGES FROM A SPACE BEING
TO THE PEOPLE OF EARTH

Paperback • 174 pages • $11.95
ISBN: 978-1-943928-10-1

R. A. Goal, a certified messiah from Planet Andalucia Beta in Ursa Minor, gives humans on Earth three predictions for 2021. They include the prospect of the novel coronavirus pandemic, the outlook of economic crisis, and the risk of war. But the hope is that Savior is now born on Earth to overcome any bad predictions. Now is the time to open our hearts and listen to the words from R. A. Goal.

THE TRUE HEART OF YAIDRON

GUIDELINES FOR HUMANKIND SUFFERING FROM THE CORONAVIRUS

Paperback • 144 pages • $11.95
ISBN: 978-1-943928-04-0

What are the real cause and evil schemes behind the worldwide coronavirus crisis? Out of compassion, this book reveals truths about the all-out global war now being waged by the evil power in East Asia that's destroying the power of the people. Discover the movement that's trying to bring together the powers of the West, India, and Asia by the belief of "With Savior," to save humankind and create the new golden future of Earth.

WITH SAVIOR

MESSAGES FROM SPACE BEING YAIDRON

Paperback • 232 pages • $13.95
ISBN: 978-1-943869-94-7

The human race is now faced with multiple unprecedented crises. Perhaps God is warning us humans to reconsider our materialistic and arrogant ways. Fortunately, God has sent us a savior, who is now teaching us to repent and showing us the path we should choose. In this book, space being Yaidron sends his warnings and messages of hope.

CONSIDERING THE FUTURE OF THE WORLD

TRUMP SHALL NEVER DIE

HIS DETERMINATION TO COME BACK

Paperback • 206 pages • $11.95
ISBN: 978-1-943928-08-8

This book unveiled Mr. Donald Trump's true thoughts never reported by the media through spiritual interview with the guardian spirit of him. The topics include the "madness" found in GAFA and the mainstream media, Mr. Trump's views on the coronavirus vaccine and global warming, and the true aim of "Make America Great Again."

THE XI JINPING THOUGHT NOW

Paperback • 212 pages • $13.95
ISBN: 978-1-943928-05-7

With the launch of Biden administration in the U.S. and the 100th anniversary of the founding of the Chinese Communist Party approaching, China has been expanding its military threat and reinforcing its influence over the world. What urges China to seek global hegemony? This book unveils the "dark being" behind the Xi Jinping Thought.

WILL THERE BE PEACE IN MYANMAR?

SPIRITUAL INTERVIEWS WITH THE GUARDIAN SPIRITS OF AUNG SAN SUU KYI AND GEN. MIN AUNG HLAING AND MESSAGES FROM SHAKYAMUNI BUDDHA

Paperback • 194 pages • $11.95
ISBN: 978-1-943928-12-5

February 2021. Tatmadaw, Myanmar Armed Forces, staged a coup against the pro-democracy leader Aung San Suu Kyi. Behind the nation's army lurks one of the world's major powers working to gain its influence on Myanmar. But, now is the time for the world to change. Words from Shakyamuni Buddha will also help bring peace to Myanmar, Asia, and the world.

BOOKS ON SURVIVING IN THE AGE OF CRISIS

ROJIN, BUDDHA'S MYSTICAL POWER

ITS ULTIMATE ATTAINMENT IN TODAY'S WORLD

Paperback • 224 pages • $16.95
ISBN: 978-1-942125-82-2

In this book, Ryuho Okawa has redefined the traditional Buddhist term *Rojin* and explained that in modern society it means the following: the ability for individuals with great spiritual powers to live in the world as people with common sense while using their abilities to the optimal level. This book will unravel the mystery of the mind and lead you to the path to enlightenment.

HOW TO BECOME A CREATIVE PERSON

Paperback • 176 pages • $16.95
ISBN: 978-1-942125-84-6

How can we become creative when we feel we are not naturally creative? This book provides easy to follow universal and hands-on-rules to become a creative person in work and life. These methods of becoming creative are certain to bring you success in work and life. Discover the secret ingredient for becoming truly creative.

THE ESSENCE OF BUDDHA

THE PATH TO ENLIGHTENMENT

Paperback • 208 pages • $14.95
ISBN: 978-1-942125-06-8

In this book, Ryuho Okawa imparts in simple and accessible language his wisdom about the essence of Shakyamuni Buddha's philosophy of life and enlightenment-teachings that have been inspiring people all over the world for over 2,500 years. By offering a new perspective on core Buddhist thoughts, Okawa brings these teachings to life for modern people. This book distills a way of life that anyone can practice to achieve a life of self-growth, compassionate living, and true happiness.

For a complete list of books, visit okawabooks.com

WHAT WILL BECOME OF CORONAVIRUS PANDEMIC?
Readings by Edgar Cayce

UFOS CAUGHT ON CAMERA!
A Spiritual Investigation on Videos and Photos of the Luminous Objects Visiting Earth

THE LAWS OF SUCCESS
A Spiritual Guide to Turning Your Hopes into Reality

THE POWER OF BASICS
Introduction to Modern Zen Life of Calm, Spirituality and Success

WORRY-FREE LIVING
Let Go of Stress and Live in Peace and Happiness

THE STRONG MIND
The Art of Building the Inner Strength to Overcome Life's Difficulties

INVINCIBLE THINKING
An Essential Guide for a Lifetime of Growth, Success, and Triumph

THINK BIG!
Be Positive and Be Brave to Achieve Your Dreams

CHANGE YOUR LIFE, CHANGE THE WORLD
A Spiritual Guide to Living Now

For a complete list of books, visit okawabooks.com

MUSIC BY RYUHO OKAWA

THE THUNDER

a composition for repelling the Coronavirus

We have been granted this music from our Lord. It will repel away the novel Coronavirus originated in China. Experience this magnificent powerful music.

Search on YouTube

the thunder coronavirus for a short ad!

THE EXORCISM

prayer music for repelling Lost Spirits

Feel the divine vibrations of this Japanese and Western exorcising symphony to banish all evil possessions you suffer from and to purify your space!

Search on YouTube

the exorcism repelling for a short ad!

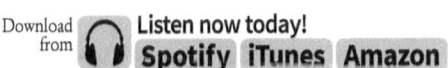

Download from **Listen now today!** **Spotify** **iTunes** **Amazon**

CD available at amazon.com, and Happy Science locations worldwide

WITH SAVIOR

English version

***"Come what may,
you shall expect your future"***

This is the message of hope to the modern people who are living in the midst of the Coronavirus pandemic, natural disasters, economic depression, and other various crises.

Search on YouTube | **with savior** | for a short ad!

THE WATER REVOLUTION

English and Chinese version

"Power to the People!"

For the truth and happiness of the 1.4 billion people in China who have no freedom. Love, justice, and sacred rage of God are on this melody that will give you courage to fight to bring peace.

Search on YouTube | **the water revolution** | for a short ad!

CD available at amazon.com, and Happy Science locations worldwide

Download from **Listen now today!** **Spotify** **iTunes** **Amazon**

www.ingramcontent.com/pod-product-compliance
Lightning Source LLC
Chambersburg PA
CBHW030153100526
44592CB00009B/257
9781943928194